TREATING ANXIETY DISORDERS

SAGE HUMAN SERVICES GUIDES, VOLUME 45

SAGE HUMAN SERVICES GUIDES

*a series of books edited by ARMAND LAUFFER and CHARLES D. GARVIN.
Published in cooperation with the University of Michigan School of Social
Work and other organizations.*

A **SAGE** HUMAN SERVICES GUIDE **45**

TREATING ANXIETY DISORDERS

A Guide for Human Service Professionals

Bruce A. THYER

Published in cooperation with the University of
Michigan School of Social Work

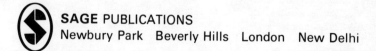

SAGE PUBLICATIONS
Newbury Park   Beverly Hills   London   New Delhi

For information address:

SAGE Publications, Inc.
2111 West Hillcrest Drive
Newbury Park, California 91320

SAGE Publications Inc.   SAGE Publications Ltd.
275 South Beverly Drive   28 Banner Street
Beverly Hills   London EC1Y 8QE
California 90212   England

SAGE PUBLICATIONS India Pvt. Ltd.
M-32 Market
Greater Kailash I
New Delhi 110 048 India

Printed in the United States of America

Library of Congress Cataloging-in-Publication Data

Main entry under title:

Thyer, Bruce A.
    Treating anxiety disorders.

    (Sage human services guides ; 45)
    "Published in cooperation with the University of
Michigan School of Social Work."
    Bibliography: p.
    1. Anxiety. 2. Phobias. 3. Anxiety—Treatment.
4. Phobias—Treatment. I. University of Michigan.
School of Social Work. II. Title. III. Series: Sage
human services guides ; v. 45. [DNLM: 1. Anxiety
Disorders—therapy. WM 172 T549t]
RC531.T48   1986   616.85'223   86-13110
ISBN 0-8039-2792-4 (pbk.)

CONTENTS

PREFACE

This book was written as an introductory clinical guide for social workers, psychologists, psychiatrists, mental health counselors, and other human service professionals who are called upon to treat clients suffering from pathological anxiety. I have found that my own clinical experience with these clients has been immensely rewarding. For most anxious individuals, the knowledgeable human service professional is in a good position to offer a significant degree of help, and such an optimistic appraisal is all too rare in the treatment of mental disorders. An attempt was made to convey the most recent advances in understanding the causes of the various anxiety disorders and in their clinical management. Working with phobic individuals and with those suffering from one of the other anxiety disorders affords the human service professional the opportunity to exercise a full repertoire of clinical skills and therapeutic modalities, including individual treatment, group therapy, psychoeducational interventions, marital and family counseling, and community networking. A good knowledge of contemporary psychoparmacological management practices relevant to the anxiety disorders is a prerequisite to helping individuals with certain of these conditions, and the human service professional lacking such expertise is urged to consult some of the primary references cited in the text covering this topic.

I would like to acknowledge my debts of gratitude to a number of individuals who in many ways made this book possible. First and foremost is the debt I owe to my clients. If I have been able to assist them to only a small proportion of the degree to which I have been professionally and personally enriched by my work with them, then I will have been amply rewarded. A number of colleagues at the University of Michigan Hospitals provided several years of intellectual challenge, clinical supervision, support, and friendship, including but not limited to George C. Curtis, Oliver G. Cameron, and Randy M. Nesse. I owe a large intellectual debt to several clinical researchers in the field of anxiety disorders whose publications have greatly influenced me, again including but not limited to Isaac M. Marks, David V. Sheehan, Donald F. Klein, and Gail S. Steketee. I have enjoyed several years of friendship and collaboration with Mary Ann Miller and her husband Bob, two remarkable individuals who virtually single-handedly founded an extremely successful agoraphobia self-help group in the Detroit metropolitan area which has been of benefit to hundreds of anxious individuals. My conversations and collaboration with Mary Ann, Bob, and the members of *Agoraphobics in Motion* have always been most rewarding and enjoyable. Throughout the composition of this book my wife Joan has been remarkably patient and understanding. Without her support and encouragement it would not have been completed. Preparation of this book was facilitated by a Florida State University Foundation 1985 summer research grant to the author.

This book is dedicated to my clients and to the past, present, and future members of A.I.M.

Tallahassee, Florida   Bruce A. Thyer

Chapter 1

NEW DEVELOPMENTS IN
THE FIELD OF ANXIETY DISORDERS

This is, I think, the age of anxiety.

—Louis Kronenberger

These are exciting times for human service professionals who treat clients suffering from the anxiety disorders. The third edition of the *Diagnostic and Statistical Manual of Mental Disorders* (DSM-III) published by the American Psychiatric Association (1980) has dramatically revised the diagnostic nomenclature and descriptive pathology for each of the major syndromes characterized by severe anxiety. Certain traditional diagnostic labels have been eliminated in favor of a newer system with a greater empirical base. It is now essential that informed human service workers have a firm grasp of the contemporary language found in the DSM-III in order to communicate effectively with their colleagues.

In 1984, researchers with the National Institute of Mental Health published the preliminary results from the first nationwide psychiatric epidemiological study and reported that the most prevalent form of mental illness in the United States is not alcoholism or the affective disorders, as previously supposed, but the anxiety disorders (Myers et al., 1984). Between 60 and 150 out of 1000 people in the three metropolitan areas surveyed are now estimated to meet the DSM-III criteria for one or more of the anxiety disorders, and less severe but still problematic anxiousness is even more common. Barlow et al. (1984) report that the Gallup survey organization, using well-validated but conservative criteria, found marked anxiety to be characteristic of 30%-40% of the general population. It has been known for years that most individuals suffering from disabling anxiety are treated by general medical practitioners and that anxiety is one of the most common diagnoses found in medical practice.

Another important development occurred with the advent of the DSM-III in 1980. An earlier draft of the manual (Task Force, 1977) was circulated across the country to selected clinical centers for field-testing purposes. The draft contained diagnostic material virtually identical to those eventually published in the final 1980 version, but it continued the practice found in the DSM-I and DSM-II of classifying all mental disorders as *medical* conditions and of asserting that psychiatrists and other medical specialists were the individuals best qualified to diagnose mental illnesses. This purely medical model of mental illness is objectionable to human service professionals such as psychologists, social workers, and psychiatric nurses, individuals often possessing years of clinical training, practice experience, and research skills in the field of mental illness. In their reaction after reviewing the 1977 draft of the DSM-III, Schacht and Nathan (1977) pointed out that few of the disorders listed in the manual had a known organic etiology, a fact also acknowledged by those instrumental in developing the draft. Spitzer and Williams (1983) note that the "DSM-III recognizes that with only a few exceptions (primarily the organic mental disorders) the etiology of mental disorders remains unknown" (p. 808). Thus according to Schacht and Nathan (1977), asserting the primacy of the medical model in mental illness was primarily a political act, not a scientifically justifiable position. As a consequence, largely due to the efforts of clinical psychologists, the final published version of the DSM-III dropped the contention that the mental illnesses represented medical disorders.

This has important repercussions for the nonmedical human service professional. Now one's ability to employ the DSM-III to diagnose mental illness is based solely upon one's competence and training in the use of the criteria, not on professional discipline. This places professionals with a background in the psychosocial sciences on a more equal footing with their medical colleagues and appropriately recognizes the valuable contributions to be made by competent psychologists, social workers, psychiatric nurses, and other human service professionals in the diagnostic process.

Since the beginning of modern theories and treatments of mental illness, the phenonemon of anxiety has been a cornerstone in the formulation and understanding of abnormal behavior. Freud's early work with the hysterical "Anna O" and the phobic "Little Hans" led him to view the experience of pathological anxiety in the form of specific phobias or nonspecific generalized anxiety as defensive mechanisms that possessed adaptive features for the individual. Indeed, the concept of anxiety became central to the understanding of all neurotic conflicts, despite the widely recognized fact that conventional dynamic psychotherapy was not an efficacious therapy for most patients suffering from clinical anxiety. The well-known conditions of agoraphobia, obsessive-compulsive disorder, anxiety states, and even monosymptomatic phobias were acknowledged to be largely intractable conditions. Freud himself is known to have suffered for years from fears of traveling.

Fortunately, the past two decades have witnessed dramatic advances in both the understanding and effective treatment of the anxiety disorders. Dozens of randomized controlled clinical trials with extensive follow-up periods and involving hundreds of patients suffering from pathological anxiety have been conducted that were devoted to the systematic development, testing, and extension of new and effective interventions. For most of the categories now found in the DSM-III chapter on anxiety disorders, specific treatments are now available to provide significant help for the majority of such patients. These treatment advances have occurred on two major fronts, the first consisting of psychological intervention largely derived from contemporary learning theory, and the second being biological, based upon the development of effective pharmacotherapy for certain of the anxiety disorders and on dramatic findings concerning the psychobiological mechanisms of severe fear.

On the psychological front, the "principle of therapeutic exposure" to anxiety-evoking stimuli has been clearly articulated, systematized, and extensively tested, resulting in the development of a variety of highly effective interventions for those disorders characterized by severe anxiety evoked by the confrontation or anticipated exposure to discrete environmental stimuli. This form of fear is characteristic of the majority of the anxiety disorders, including simple phobia, social phobia, agoraphobia, obsessive-compulsive disorder, and some patients with panic disorder—individuals who form the bulk of those suffering from pathological anxiety. There is also encouraging evidence that this principle of therapeutic exposure can be successfully applied to treat individuals who are troubled not by fears of external stimuli but by internal stimuli such as obsessional thoughts or frightening somatic sensations.

Another group of patients suffer from severe fear that is *not* evoked by discrete environmental stimuli or thoughts but from paroxysmal episodes of acute anxiety or panic that occur without warning. This is particularly troubling not only because of the terrifying nature of these panic attacks themselves but also because the individual often develops severe generalized, pervasive, or anticipatory anxiety, dreading yet not knowing when the next panic attack will strike. The experience of spontaneous panic attacks is central to diagnoses of panic disorder, agoraphobia with panic attacks, certain individuals with apparent generalized anxiety disorder, and simple or social phobias. As will be reviewed in the relevent chapters, there now exist specific and effective antipanic medications, which, if conscientiously taken on a regular basis, completely block the occurrence of spontaneous panic attacks. This is encouraging news in light of the fact that there are no known psychosocial treatments that have been clearly shown to prevent spontaneous panic attacks. Now, however, most individuals suffering from such episodes of panic, when appropriately treated with medication, can enjoy a life free from such disabling attacks and the resultant "fear of fear."

Related developments in biological psychiatry strongly suggest that spontaneous panic attacks may be the result of an inherited metabolic disorder. This research, reviewed in Chapter 3, has offered dramatic new insights into the phenomenology and descriptive pathology of panic attacks, brings a sense of order to a highly complex set of interwoven symptoms, and serves to make sense of a perplexing constellation of somatic and psychological complaints that have served to bewilder clinicians for decades.

Prior to exploring each of the above issues, it is worthwhile to note the adaptive nature of fear.

FUNCTIONAL ANXIETY

In common with all other aspects of human structure and function, the capacity to experience anxiety undoubtedly represents an evolved adaptive mechanism that enhances the survival of our species. Far from being a psychopathological process, for most individuals anxiety serves to motivate constructive activity. Millenia ago our ancestors found anxiety to be a neccessary preparatory stimulus for flight or to fight. Each of the characteristics of severe anxiety served a useful function. Hyperventilation oxygenated the blood; perspiration cooled the body and made it more difficult to be grasped or abraded; peripheral vasoconstriction (cold extremities) shunted blood away from the skin and into the deeper musculature to provide added endurance; heart rate and blood pressure increases also set the stage for sustained physical exertion. In contemporary life we are largely free from attack by carnivorous predators, yet we display reactions similar to such threats when we are confronted with situations such as public speaking or passing an important examination. For most individuals, milder forms of anxiety stimulate adaptive or preparatory responses such as rehearsing one's speech or industriously studying prior to an examination. Likewise, anxiety motivates us to avoid the vicious dog, steer clear of the edge of the cliff, or securely lock our doors at night prior to retiring. The effect of anxiety on adaptive performance ranges from the completely apathetic person who fails to undertake necessary action, to the moderately apprehensive person adequately preparing to meet necessary challenges, and, at the far extreme, the person so incapacitated by fear as to become completely immobilized. It is this latter category of individuals who are subsumed under the DSM-III chapter on anxiety disorders and who form the focus of this book.

A considerable body of research, largely conducted by developmental psychologists, clearly demonstrates that certain forms of fearful behavior are normal and predictable stages that can be expected to occur in children and adolescents. The newborn infant possesses several innate fearful reactions, such as to loud noises and to the sudden loss of support. From ages 1 through 4 years, fearful reactions upon being separated from one's parent(s) or primary caregiver are common, as are fears of strangers and darkness. With time these fears usually cease to be displayed and others may make their appearance. For example, the school-age child reports an increasing preoccupation with fears centered on social situations, school performance, and physical appearance, whereas by this time the child has usually lost stranger and separation fears and fears of certain animals, such as dogs, cats, snakes, and insects. More detailed information on the various categories of age-related fears and their expected dates of emergence and disappearance can be found in most contemporary textbooks in developmental psychology and in the original studies reporting these findings.

NONFUNCTIONAL ANXIETY

When anxiety exists to such a degree that an individual's psychosocial functioning has become significantly impaired, the response has lost its adaptive characteristics and becomes nonfunctional or pathological in nature. By definition, phobias are irrational responses, out of proportion to the demands of the situation, that cannot be explained or reasoned away and lead to avoidance whenever possible. If a person is fearful of an object, animal, or situation that is rarely encountered, the degree of disability may be quite small. But all too often the human service professional encounters clients whose fears dominate their lives to such an extent that their work and social functioning are significantly impaired. One client I knew had such an excessive fear of encountering roaches that she committed suicide rather than live a life filled with the constant dread of seeing the horrible insects. This tragic outcome was particularly remarkable because the client was not significantly depressed and not suffering from a psychotic disorder.

The anxiety disorders are receiving an increasing degree of publicity in the form of articles and stories appearing in leading magazines and national newspapers. For example, the November 23, 1984 issue of *Newsweek* had as its cover story, "Phobias: New Drugs and Therapies for Helping People Conquer Their Fear." Shorter articles on panic disorder and phobias appeared in *U.S. News and World Report* in 1980 and 1981, and a November 1983 cover story for the Sunday magazine *Family Weekly* was entitled, "Fears and Phobias: New Ways to Fight Fright." Both the *New York Times* and *U.S.A. Today* have periodically featured the anxiety disorders in their human interest sections in recent years, and short articles frequently appear in various health and women's magazines. October 1985 was designated by the U.S. Congress as "Phobia Awareness Month," and congressional testimony by leading experts on the prevalence and treatment of the anxiety disorders was given widespread publicity. In addition, both of the leading television "news magazines," *60 Minutes* and *20-20*, have featured phobias and other anxiety disorders on their programs within the last two years.

Such publicity is serving to educate the general public about the nature, prevalence, and treatment of the anxiety disorders, and the developing interest in these conditions is prompting a great increase in the number of individuals seeking effective treatment for their fears. As a consequence, a growing number of specialty clinics have been established in the past decade explicitly devoted to treating the anxious client. Originally such clinics were almost exclusively affiliated with major research institutions such as universities, medical schools, or hospitals, but more and more free-standing anxiety clinics are being formed. A glance through the "yellow pages" of most larger cities will reveal the number of social workers, psychologists, and psychiatrists who specify that they offer specific treatment for phobias and other anxiety-related conditions.

Our own Anxiety Disorders Program at the University of Michigan Hospitals had a clinical staff of one social worker (the author), four board-certified faculty psychiatrists, several psychiatric residents, and one or two psychology or social work interns. Despite this level of staffing, our waiting period rarely dipped below six months and usually involved 100-200 potential clients. During one two-week period following a television interview in Detroit with the author we added 60 new referrals to our waiting list. All these factors suggest that the competent human service professional will have little trouble finding an adequate caseload of clients suffering from pathological anxiety.

A number of self-help groups are currently established throughout the United States, usually run by recovered agoraphobics and often with professional advisement. A new national organization, the Phobia Society of America (PSA), was formed several years ago. Membership is open to human service professionals with an interest in the anxiety disorders and to anxious individuals themselves. Local chapters of the PSA have been formed across the country, the organization sponsors an annual convention devoted to scientific research and clinical issues germaine to the anxiety disorders, and the group publishes a newsletter called the *Fear Breaker*. The PSA also maintains a registry of human service professionals offering specialized treatment for anxious individuals. To contact the PSA, write to The Phobia Society of America, 5820 Hubbard Drive, Rockville, Maryland 20852.

Chapter 2

SIMPLE AND SOCIAL PHOBIAS
Diagnosis, Description, and Etiology

My apprehensions come in crowds; I dread the rustling of the grass;
The very shadows of the clouds, have power to shake me as they pass.
—William Wordsworth, *1804*

Phobos was a minor Greek diety who served as an attendent to Ares, the god of war. Prior to going into battle, Greek soldiers would afix fierce images of Phobos to the front of their shields, whose visage was intended to strike their opponents with dread and fear, causing them to flee. Literary references to individuals possessing severe yet unreasonable fears are plentiful. Soranus of Ephesus (ca. A.D. 100) described a person with a morbid fear of falling into ditches (see Ackernecht, 1968). The earliest known use of the term *phobia* to refer to irrational fears also occurred during the first century A.D., by the Roman writer Celsus, who coined the word *hydrophobia* to describe the aversion to drinking water, which is symptomatic of rabies (see Gray, 1978).

The modern use of the term *phobia* was formally established in 1871 by the German physician Carl Westphal, who defined *agoraphobia* as a fear of assembly or of meeting in public places, a descriptive error that has continued until the present day, as will be seen in Chapter 4. Other phobias soon followed. The Italian psychiatrist Raggi is credited with the first use of term *claustrophobia* in 1877, referring to a morbid fear of enclosed places or confinement (Gray, 1978, p. 134), and Kraepelin included phobias as a diagnostic category in his classic 1883 textbook on psychopathology. In 1897 the American psychiatrist G. Stanley Hall published a long list of the so-called phobias, consisting of words constructed by attaching a Greek prefix to the root word "phobia." This practice was continued in 1902 by Pitres and Regis, who presented a list of 70 such phobias (see Lewis, 1976). Most contemporary psychology textbooks and popular press articles describing phobias contain a selective list of irrational fears, usually chosen because of their bizzare nature and intended to amuse the sophisticated reader.

This practice of creating long lists of phobias is unfortunate for several reasons. It develops a system of categorization that, rather than subsuming disorders with a common etiology or symptomatic profile under a broader diagnostic label, tends to encourage the proliferation of more and more categories. Thus while the pretense of science is maintained, in actuality this so-called diagnostic system is of little practical value, emphasizing the surface *differences* between types of fears rather than pointing out their underlying similarities. A further drawback is that this lexicographical approach fails to provide the human service professional with any information or guidance on the development of appropriate treatment plans.

Freud (1894/1955a, 1926/1959) tried to reverse this trend by postulating that there were only three major types of phobias, arrived at by a rationale assessment of the degree of objective threat or danger presented. The first category of fears consisted of those situations that objectively contained a reasonable amount of danger and were akin to the fearful experiences of normal people. The second category of phobias concerned fears of situations in which there was some mild element of danger but the individual's fearful response was out of proportion to the demands of the situation. Examples of this type of phobia would be a person afraid of traveling by train or of walking along a crowded street. The third category of phobias consisted of completely inappropriate fears in situations with little or no objective danger, such as fears of small harmless animals (e.g., kittens) or situations (e.g., walking across an empty street or going into shops). Freud's influence is apparent in a recent (but since superseded) definition of phobic neurosis as "characterized by intense fear of an object or situation which the patient consciously recognizes as no real danger to him" (American Psychiatric Association, 1968).

In 1980, the American Psychiatric Association published its revised set of diagnostic criteria for the phobic disorders, subdivided into *Simple Phobia, Social Phobia,* and *Agoraphobia*, with or without panic attacks, presented in Table 1. Due to its complexity, agoraphobia will be discussed in Chapter 4. Under this system, known as the *Diagnostic and Statistical Manual of Mental Disorders*, third edition (DSM-III), any present manifestation of irrational fear, if coupled with avoidance and evoked by specific environmental stimuli, is labeled as either a simple or social phobia (American Psychiatric Association, 1980). The only difference between the two diagnoses is in the nature of the external anxiety-evoking stimulus. Specifically, if the anxiety-evoking stimulus involves exposure to the scrutiny of others, liberally interpreted, the client is diagnosed as a social phobic. By definition, all remaining fears,

Table 1:   DSM-III Criteria for Simple and Social Phobia

Criterion A	
Simple Phobia	A persistent, irrational fear of, and compelling desire to avoid, an object or situation other than being alone, or in public places away from home (agoraphobia), or of humiliation or embarrassment in certain social situations (social phobia). Phobic objects are often animals, and phobic situations frequently involve heights or closed spaces.
Social phobia	A persistent, irrational fear of, and compelling desire to avoid, a situation in which the individual is exposed to possible scrutiny by others and fears that he or she will act in a way that will be humiliating or embarrassing.
Criterion B	
Simple and Social phobia	Significant distress from the disturbance and recognition that his or her fear is excessive or unreasonable.
Criterion C	
Simple and Social phobia	Not due to another mental disorder (i.e, schizophrenia, obsessive-compulsive disorder, major depression, avoidant personality disorder).

SOURCE: American Psychiatric Association (1980, pp. 228-230).

except for those subsumed under the agoraphobic diagnoses, are diagnosed as simple phobia. Because of the similarity of these two disorders, they are presented and discussed together in this chapter.

DESCRIPTIVE FEATURES

Simple and social phobias probably represent the most prevalent mental disorders in the general population, yet they appear relatively infrequently for treatment at community mental health centers, with private practitioners, or in hospital clinics. This is probably because, albeit with some difficulty, phobic encounters can often be avoided. If, however, the phobic object, animal, or situation is common, impairment may be considerable and clients can experience severe restrictions in their comfort and freedom of movement. As most instances of simple and social phobia have their onset during the childhood or teenage years, the adult phobic may have resigned himself or herself to simply living with the discomfort associated with their fears, perhaps rationalizing it with thoughts such as, "I am just an especially shy or modest person" in the case of social phobia, or "I have always been afraid of thus and so and I guess I'll never change."

One major epidemiological study estimated the prevalence of phobias in the general population as 77/1000 people, although only

9/1000 had ever seen a psychiatrist for the treatment of a phobia (Agras, Sylvester & Oliveau, 1969). The more recent epidemiological study on psychiatric conditions conducted by researchers with the National Institute of Mental Health (Myers et al., 1984) found the anxiety disorders to be the *most common* mental disorder in the United States. Their preliminary findings have not reported the exact proportion of these who are simple or social phobics, however.

Studies by developmental psychologists have documented the existence of age-related fears that may reach phobiclike proportions, occurring in a large percentage of children and at fairly predictable times (Ilg & Ames, 1955; Jersild, 1968; Kellerman, 1981; Lapouse & Monk, 1959). The newborn infant comes equipped with several innate fear reactions, such as to loud noises and to the sudden loss of support. In the early childhood years, marked fears of strangers, darkness, animals, or separation from one's parents often make their appearance, only to dissipate with the passage of time. In the school-age child and early adolescent, one often sees an increasing preoccupation with fears centered on social situations, school performance, or physical appearance. Abe and Masui (1981) found that fears of being looked at and fears of blushing peaked during adolescence and occurred, on the average, about two years earlier in girls than in boys. It should be emphasized that these age-related fears are usually transitory and almost always resolve themselves without any professional intervention—or, for that matter, parental action (Agras et al., 1972). Morris and Kratochwill (1983) suggest that parental concern over these fears is warranted only if the fear is (1) severe, (2) lasts over a relatively long period of time, and (3) creates problems in living for the child and/or parent(s).

In contrast to the relatively favorable prognosis of childhood fears and phobias, those youthful fears that persist into adulthood or have their origin during the adult years have a poor prognosis. In a group of untreated adult phobics assessed over a five-year period, Agras et al. (1972) found that only 6% became free from their fears, whereas 37% actually experienced an intensification of their phobias.

In the Anxiety Disorders Program at the University of Michigan, unlike in a general psychiatric practice, a large number of simple and social phobics appeared requesting treatment, totaling several hundred people over a five-year period. This suggests that the establishment of reputable specialty clinics providing effective treatment of phobias and the other anxiety disorders can motivate such patients actively to seek relief from their fears.

The DSM-III states that simple phobia is diagnosed more frequently in females than in males, but it fails to provide any information of the sex ratio occurring in social phobia. Age of onset in social phobia is often late childhood and early adolescence, whereas simple phobias are known to develop at any age, although most animal phobias first appear during the early childhood years (American Psychiatric Association, 1980, pp. 227-229). In our clinic 72% of our simple phobics were women, whereas 52% of the social phobics were female, suggesting that the phenomenon of social anxiety is more evenly distributed between the genders than other focal fears. Information on the ages of onset of these two conditions is presented in Table 2 and Figures 1 and 2. Note that these data were all retrospectively obtained from adult phobics. Also note that the mean ages of onset for the two disorders are virtually identical but the patterns of the histograms plotting these ages of onset are somewhat different, reflecting the previously noted observation that most simple phobias have their onset in early childhood, whereas social phobias usually emerge during the school-age years. The data in Table 2 and Figures 1 and 2 were obtained from patients seen in our clinic and previously published in Thyer, Parrish, Curtis, Cameron, and Nesse (1985).

For years clinical folklore has suggested that adult women are generally more fearful than adult men. Most past research on the topic has indeed found that, statistically, females do score significantly higher on fear questionnaries than males (Bernstein & Allen, 1969; Geer, 1965; Hersen, 1973; Manesevitz & Lanyon, 1965; Wilson, 1967) and that this difference appears as early as 9-12 years of age (Scherer & Nakamura, 1968). We attempted to replicate some of these findings using a sample of 104 clinically anxious women and 37 clinically anxious men who sought treatment at our hospital and met the DSM-III criteria for one of the anxiety disorders. Each patient completed, as a part of the intake process, the well-validated Fear Survey Schedule (FSS) by Wolpe and Lang (1977), which asks the respondent to rate how fearful they are of 108 potential anxiety-evoking objects, animals, or situations. The total FSS score represents an overall measure of anxiety and specific fears. In fact, we did *not* find women to score significantly higher than the men, and overall there was a remarkable degree of similarity between the patterns of fears reported by the two genders. For example, the ten most fear-provoking stimuli as separately rated by the men and women are displayed in Table 3. This table demonstrates that the two groups rated the same nine items among the ten most frightening situations or experiences they could encounter, a striking degree of similarity when it is realized that these ten items were derived from a pool of 108 possible

Table 2:   Age of Onset Information for Simple and Social Phobia

Diagnosis	Number of Patients	Median Age of Onset (years)	Mean Age of Onset (years)	Standard Deviation
Simple phobia	152	12	16.1	11.5
Social phobia	42	15	15.7	8.5

SOURCE: Data obtained from Thyer, Parrish, Cameron, and Nesse (1985).

Table 3:   Rankings of the Top Ten Fears of 141 Anxious Patients

Rank	Females (n = 104)	Males (n = 37)
1st	Prospect of a surgical operation	Speaking in public
2nd	Speaking in public	Losing control of yourself
3rd	Losing control of yourself	Failure
4th	Feeling rejected by others	Feeling rejected by others
5th	Failure	Looking foolish
6th	Looking down from high buildings	Prospect of a surgical operation
7th	Looking foolish	Feeling disapproved of
8th	Hurting the feelings of others	Hurting the feelings of others
9th	Journeys by airplane	Looking down from high buildings
10th	Feeling disapproved of	Thoughts of being mentally ill

SOURCE: Data obtained from Thyer, Tomlin, Curtis, Cameron, and Nesse (1985).

fear-evoking cues. Moreover, the men and women did not significantly differ in the severity of their fear scores for any of the nine conguent items. These results suggest that clinically anxious men and women possess more similarities than differences with respect to the types of stimuli they fear, and that few *clinically* meaningful gender differences exist with respect to overall fearfulness. Earlier studies that found such differences tended to report findings derived from college student samples, and such results do not appear relevant to clinical populations of anxious patients. Additional details on this study may be found in Thyer et al. (1985).

COMPLICATIONS OF SIMPLE OR SOCIAL PHOBIAS

Clinical lore (Calef, 1967; Curlee & Stern, 1973; Kraft, 1971; Marks, 1969) and some controlled research (Mullaney & Trippett, 1979; Smail, Stockwell, Canter, & Hodgson, 1984; Stockwell, Smail, Hodgson, & Canter, 1984) has suggested that phobic patients may run a high risk for the development of alcohol abuse, usually established after repeated attempts at self-medication with alcohol in an attempt to decrease anxiety. The DSM-III lists alcohol abuse as a possible complication for social phobia and agoraphobia, and the picture of the individual fearful

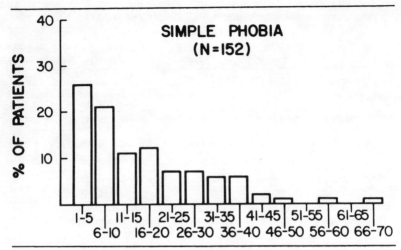

Figure 1. Distribution of the ages of onset (in five-year time periods) for 152 patients with simple phobia. From Thyer, Parrish, Curtis, Cameron, and Nesse (1985, p. 118).

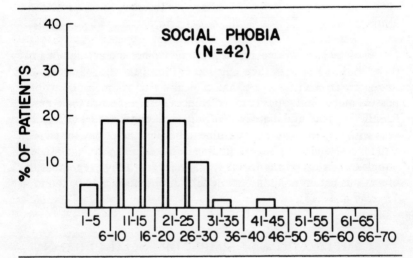

Figure 2. Distribution of the ages of onset (in five-year time periods) for 42 patients with social phobia. From Thyer, Parrish, Curtis, Cameron, and Nesse (1985, p. 118).

of flying or of public speeches having a few fortifying drinks prior to a flight or giving an address is well known. The human service professional treating clients with phobias should be alert to the possibility of such abuse because this may require professional intervention in its own right (Quitkin, Rifkin, Kaplan, & Klein, 1972). Paradoxically, controlled studies reveal that moderate ethanol intoxication does *not* provide the simple phobic with much relief from fear when encountering a fearful situation (Rimm, Briddle, Zimmerman, & Caddy, 1981; Thyer & Curtis, 1984) and may actually *impair* the possibility of their becoming more comfortable (Cameron, Curtis, Liepman, & Thyer, in press).

Occasionally the human service professional hears phobics express the concern that they might faint, die from fright, or go crazy if they ever found themselves facing what they feared with no possibility of escape. Such fears are unwarranted, with one exception. A fainting response as a component to a phobic reaction is almost exclusively limited to those clients with fears of the sight of blood or receiving injections (Connolly, Hallam, & Marks, 1976; Curtis & Thyer, 1983; Thyer, Himle, & Curtis, 1985). This reaction is due to a vasovagal response, characterized by an initial elevation in pulse and blood pressure followed by an abrupt and dramatic drop, resulting in diminished blood flow to the brain and the resultant faint (Thyer & Curtis, 1984). The reaction is usually harmless and self-regulating, in that when the individual lies down blood flow to the brain is quickly restored, leaving the person quite shaken and upset but otherwise unharmed. Individuals with other types of fears, such as public speaking, performance anxiety in musicians, heights, enclosures, or even small animals, often *feel* like they may faint, but practically speaking the risk is nil.

The notion that severe anxiety may cause one to lose control totally or "go crazy" is not limited to phobics. Some human service professionals themselves may be unsure as to what might happen—for example, "social workers are fearful of anxiety [in their clients] as if it portends an imminent breakthrough of a psychosis" (Grinker, MacGregor, Selan, Klein, & Kohrman, 1961, p. 312). Such concerns are clearly unwarranted, whether held by anxious clients or the professionals responsible for their care. To my knowledge there are no documented case examples in the professional literature describing how a simple or social phobic became so frightened that he or she died or developed a psychosis. Such *feelings* may occur, but they have no basis in fact.

The most serious complication experienced by simple or social phobics most likely involves their strenuous efforts to avoid phobic stimuli and with the debilitating anticipatory anxiety centered on *future* encounters with what they fear. Some phobics are fortunate enough to have fears of stimuli that are rarely encountered, such as the city dweller with a fear of snakes. But depending on the severity of such fears, the objectively low probability of such contact may not be sufficiently reassuring. I have seen clinical snake phobics go into paroxysms of terror and hysterical flight after seeing a *photograph* of a snake, and in one case the client coerced her husband into carefully searching the bedding and dresser drawers every night prior to retiring in order to reassure her that no serpent had slithered into their bedroom while she was at work. Before succumbing to the temptation to dynamically interpret the latter case, it is worth noting that this client and her husband both pursued successful business careers, had a warm and happy marriage with several children, and enjoyed a satisfactory sex life.

It is important for the human service professional not to be deceived by the diagnostic label of *simple* phobia into thinking this means the fear is uncomplicated or does not seriously handicap the individual concerned. Simple phobia merely indicates that the focus of the phobic reaction is based upon anxiety-evoking stimuli located in the patient's external environment. This may present as a circumscribed and limited response, *or* it may have a dramatic and pervasive impact on every aspect of the client's life.

Generally speaking, it is the social phobic who is more likely to be seriously handicapped by his or her fears, due to the ubiquitousness of social stimuli in everyday life. Typically the social phobic presents for treatment because of severe public speaking fears, which is the highest-ranked fear for most anxious patients (see Table 3), performance anxiety (as in musicians or college students facing examinations), or psychogenic urinary retention. Less common forms of social phobia include individuals unable to eat in public restaurants, an inability to engage in handwriting in public, extreme discomfort at parties or other social gatherings, and heterosocial anxiety.

As with simple phobia, the adverse effects of marked social fears can be quite extensive. Enough of us have had a taste of public speaking fears so as to be able to empathize well with the speech phobic; and for the sufferer whose job responsibilities require frequent public presentations, his or her entire life can be consumed in the anxious anticipation of the next engagement. Frequent accompaniments to the subjective fears of the social phobic are marked tremors, excessive perspiration, blushing, tremulous speech, and partial or complete aphonia. The musician or stage performer may experience similar terrors, even though the social phobic reaction may be unrelated to the performer's objective ability to perform. In a recent segment of the television program *Sixty-Minutes*, the distinguished actor Sir Lawrence Olivier gave a moving account of his experience with severe stage fright which developed, for the first time, when he was in his 60s.

Anxious students faced with examinations have been known to drop out of school or experience nightmares and insomnia during the evening prior to scheduled tests. Academic performance is frequently impaired due to test anxiety (Papsdorf, Himle, McCann, & Thyer, 1982; Thyer & Papsdorf, 1982) and student reports of "blanking out" or "freezing up" are common.

In psychogenic urinary retention the social phobic is unable to void urine in lavatories where he or she might be seen or heard by a fellow occupant or where the possibility exists of someone entering the lavatory while the phobic is attempting to void. Typically the coping mechanism engaged in by these individuals is to avoid or reduce fluid intake during the day while at work or otherwise in public and to retain urine until a safe return to home is achieved where privacy is assured. Avoidance of urination by these patients for up to 48 hours has been reported (Lamontagne & Marks, 1973) if a private bathroom is not accessible. The phobic's social life can be greatly inconvenienced by these restrictions, which occur regardless of the degree of urinary urgency or bladder pain. It has been reported that in extreme cases frequent urinary catheterization is required (Campbell, 1982) although this is not common. It should be emphasized that a diagnosis of a social phobia, as manifested by involuntary retention, is appropriate only in the absence of organic pathology. Such an absence is usually not difficult to confirm due to the unique situational specificity of the involuntary retention.

PSYCHOBIOLOGY OF PHOBIC ANXIETY

Apart from subjective fear and overt avoidance, a major component of the phobic syndrome is marked physiological arousal. Scientific research aside, there exist numerous literary references of the somatic reactions associated with severe fear. Shakespeare alone provides a comprehensive list, including the following:

Perspiration and tremor: "I am surprised with an uncouth fear/A chilling sweat o'er-runs my trembling joints" (*Titus Andronicus*).

Tachycardia and palpitations: "And make my seated heart knock at my ribs, against the use of nature" (*Macbeth*).

Peripheral vasoconstriction: "Pale as a shirt, his knees knocking each other" (*Hamlet*); "Thou tremblest; and the whiteness of thy cheek/Is apter than thy tongue to tell thy errand" (*Henry IV*).

Weakness: "Distill'd almost to jelly with the act of fear" (*Hamlet*).

Vasovagal fainting: "Many will swoon when they do see blood" (*As You Like It*).

Chills and piloerection: "I would a tale unfold whose lightest word/would harrow up thy soul, freeze thy young blood,/Make thy two eyes, like stars, start from their spheres,/Thy knotted and combined locks to part/An each particular hair to stand on end,/Like quills upon the fretful porpentine" (*Hamlet*).

Far from being a caricature drawn from an episode of *The Little Rascals*, the above descriptions have proven to be amazingly accurate, supported by numerous recent research studies. The anxious individual is known to display a simultaneous increase in heart rate and decrease in blood flow to the extremities (Thyer, Papsdorf, Davis, & Vallecorsa, 1984), and the selective association between fainting and blood phobia was only recently demonstrated (Connolly et al., 1976; Thyer, Himle, & Curtis, 1985).

Of equal interest have been recent studies on the hormonal changes associated with phobic anxiety. For most such studies the research strategy involves exposing simple or socially phobic individuals to their unique anxiety-evoking stimulus while periodically taking blood samples from an indwelling needle taped in place on the forearm. These blood samples are subsequently analyzed to determine the levels of the particular hormones of interest. Detailed comparisons can be made, for example, of the changes in adrenaline levels occurring between periods of quiet rest versus acute phobic anxiety. In the most comprehensive such study to date, Nesse et al. (1985) obtained periodic blood samples from ten women with severe phobias to small animals. The experiment consisted of four three-hour sessions; during sessions 1 and 4 the patient quietly rested in an easy chair reading magazines for three hours. During sessions 2 and 3 the first hour was also spent in quiet reading but the second hour was spent with the patient experiencing controlled yet intimate exposure to the phobic animal, such as a dog, cat, snake, or bird. This procedure, done with the patient's informed consent and without tricks or surprises, is nevertheless capable of inducing states of sheer terror under controlled laboratory conditions. After 60 minutes of such exposure, the third hour again was spent with the patient engaged in quiet reading. This experience of phobic anxiety was found to produce significant increases in the patient's pulse rate and blood pressure, and plasma levels of adrenaline, noradrenaline, cortisol, growth hormone, and insulin, all compounds produced by the body when the "fight or flight" response is engaged.

Similar findings have been reported in the controlled induction of public speaking fear in social phobics as well (Dimsdale & Moss, 1980; Moss & Wynar, 1970). Such studies emphatically point out that phobic symptomatology is not simply the whining of anxious neurotics seeking attention but actually a very real and profound bodily response with dramatic physiological effects, as if one's body is gearing up for great exertion yet little overt action is feasible.

ETIOLOGY

Over the years a wide variety of explanations for the origins of simple and social phobias have been proposed. Unfortunately, empirical inquiry has been greatly exceeded by speculation. A number of the more common proposals designed to account for irrational fears are listed in Table 4 and will be reviewed below.

Psychodynamic Factors. Although a wide variety of psychodynamic explanations have been developed to account for simple and social phobias, the final formulation arrived at by Freud (1926/1959) has remained central to such perspectives:

> Freud viewed the phobic neurosis as resulting from conflicts centered on an unresolved childhood oedipal situation. In the adult, the sexual drive continues to have a strong incestuous coloring, and its arousal tends to arouse anxiety. The anxiety then alerts the ego to exert repression to keep the drive away from conscious representation and discharge. When repression fails to be entirely successful in its function, the ego must call on auxiliary defenses. In phobic patients, these defenses involve primarily the use of displacement. The sexual conflict is displaced from the person who evokes the conflict to a seemingly unimportant, irrelevant object or situation, which now has the power to arouse the entire constellation of affects, including signal anxiety. The phobic object or situation selected usually has a direct associative connection with the primary source of the conflict. Furthermore, the situation or object is usually such that the patient is able to keep out of its way." (Freedman, Kaplan, & Sadock, 1976, pp. 625-626)

Symbolism is thus the major explanatory concept to account for the specificity of simple and social phobias. For example,

> Phobias about infection and touching often express the need to avoid dirt and show that the patient has to defend himself against anal-erotic

Table 4:   Hypothetical Etiologies for Simple and Social Phobias

Psychodynamic factors (unresolved Oedipal conflicts, and others)
Phylogenetic influences
Observational learning (modeling)
Psychological factors (e.g., irrational thinking)
Respondent conditioning (direct trauma)
Positive reinforcement (secondary gain?)
Negative reinforcement (serves to maintain phobic avoidance?)

temptation. Fear of open streets and stage fright may be defenses against exhibitionistic wishes. Anxiety about high places, closed places, fallings, cars, trains and airplanes are developed to fight pleasurable sensations connected with stimulation involving equilibrium." (Freedman et al., 1976, p. 259)

According to this perspective, psychoanalysis or psychodynamic psychotherapy would be necessary to resolve successfully the intrapsychic conflicts producing phobic symptomatology. Unfortunately, there is almost complete agreement among authorities in the field that such therapies are ineffective in the treatment of phobias, and there do not yet exist controlled clinical trials demonstrating that dynamically oriented therapies provide relief from irrational fears. Freud himself noted, "One can hardly ever master a phobia if one waits till the patient lets the analysis influence him to give it up" (1897/1955, p. 155), and earlier stated that phobic anxiety "proves not irreducible further by psychological analysis, and is also not amenable to psychotherapy" (1894/1955a, p. 84).

It should be clearly noted that the absence of controlled research supporting the validity of psychodynamic explanations for simple and social phobias does not, in itself, justify repudiation of such theories. The absence of evidence is not evidence of absence. Certainly dynamics such as unresolved oedipal conflicts as in Freud's analysis of "Little Hans" *may* underlie *some* instances of specific phobias, although the fact that psychodynamic therapy is apparently not an effective treatment for these disorders would appear to disconfirm these theories. The onus is clearly on the proponents of dynamic approaches to develop an adequate research base as to justify retention among contemporary theoretical formulations. This does not appear likely. It was only with the greatest of difficulty that the psychoanalytic establishment succeeded in preventing the term "neurosis" from being dropped from the nomenclature in the DSM-III (Bayer & Spitzer, 1985).

Phylogenetic Influences. As noted earlier, human infants seem to be born with at least two specific fears, to loud noises and to falling. Experiments with the "visual cliff," a table top, half of which consists of a sturdy glass plate through which can be seen a drop of several feet, clearly show that most infants at the crawling stage will avoid going over the edge, apparently reflecting a fear of heights. As infants grow older, other age-related fears make their appearance and disappearance in a fairly predictable manner. These facts have lead to speculation that humans as a species are genetically predisposed to fear certain classes of stimuli.

There are numerous infrahuman analogies. Monkeys display panic-like reactions and avoidance to the sight of snakes, even if the primates have been bred in captivity (Yerkes & Yerkes, 1936). Baby birds will escape under cover if the shadow of a preylike bird is projected overhead (Tinbergen, 1951). See Marks (1969) for a detailed presentation of similar examples of such "prepared" fears.

Other researchers have observed that the types of anxiety-evoking stimuli that appear most frequently among simple phobics appear to be classes of animals or situations that may possess some type of biological significance for the human species. These theorists note that the most common phobias are to animals such as snakes, bees, wasps, small carnivores such as dogs and cats, and spiders. Other common fears in children and adults are to heights, darkness, and enclosed spaces. Is it possible that these stimuli are feared by contemporary man because, in ages past, those ancestors of ours who successfully avoided such situations or animals were morely likely to survive long enough to reproduce, passing such avoidance patterns on to their descendents?

It is impossible to test such a theory directly (Seligman, 1971), but a series of studies by a Scandinavian research center seems to support indirectly the "preparedness hypothesis." It has been shown that in the laboratory it is easier to experimentally induce "mini-phobias" in human volunteers by pairing electric shock with the presentation of biologically "relevant" stimuli (e.g., pictures of snakes or spiders) than to biologically "irrelevant" stimuli (e.g., pictures of flowers or mushrooms; see Ohman, Eriksson, & Olofsson, 1975). Furthermore, these fear responses conditioned to biologically relevant stimuli are more difficult to decondition than fears conditioned to biologically irrelevant stimuli (Hygge & Ohman, 1978; Hugdahl, 1978). The evidence is mixed, however, in that it has been shown clinically that phobic patients with such biologically relevant fears do not require a longer period to treat effectively than patients with biologically irrelevant fears. Thus although the theory that phylogenetic influences may pertain to the etiology of certain human phobias, the notion need not influence the treatment of such clients.

A recent study supportive of the role of phylogenetic influences on human phobias was conducted by Torgersen (1979), employing a sample of 99 same-sexed pairs of twins. About half of the sample pairs were monozygotic twins and half were dyzygotic twins. Responses to a fear questionnaire by the twins revealed that both animal and social fears were more concordant among the monozygotic twins than the dyzygotic siblings—evidence, according to Torgersen, of the role genetic factors play in the development of phobic fears.

Observational Learning. It has been known for years than phobics disproportionately tend to have parents suffering from similar fears (Hagman, 1932; John, 1941), which suggests the possible role that observational learning may play in the genesis of phobias. Specifically, exposure to fearful and avoidant behavior displayed by someone else may prove to be involved in the acquisition of phobic behavior, just as learning by imitation has been shown to be a potent source of acquiring many other forms of behavior (Bandura & Walters, 1963). More direct evidence in support of this view, apart from the correlational studies mentioned above, has recently been published by Ost and Hugdahl in Sweden. In their original report (Ost & Hugdahl, 1981) a sample of 106 simple and social phobics were carefully evaluated in terms of how they acquired their irrational fears. Of the patients, 17% ascribed the onset of their fears to traumatic but *vicarious* experiences, such as seeing someone else bitten by a dog, leading to the development of a dog phobia in the observer. An additional 10% reported that their fears were established via informational or instructional processes (e.g., "Stay away from dogs, they can attack you!"). In a subgroup of simple phobics, those with fears of the dentist and to the sight of blood, Ost and Hugdahl (1985) found that 20% of their sample (total n = 73) implicated vicarious trauma in the onset of their fears—for example, seeing an accident or hearing a dental patient moan with pain. With a group of insect phobics, Fazio (1972) found that 19% reported their fears were caused by frightening information given to them by their mother. Among college students reporting dental fears (n = 487), Kleinknecht, Klepac, and Alexander (1973) reported that "negative expectancies from others" was the reported origin for the fears of 17% of their sample, a proportion similar to that found by Bernstein, Kleinknecht, and Alexander (1979) in a sample of 225 undergraduate students.

Despite the limitations of such self-report information, it seems that vicarious exposure to traumatic experiences and/or the receipt of frightening information about specific objects, animals, or situations may set the stage for the subsequent development of a clinical phobia. Undoubtedly cultural norms and the media play roles in this process. Comic strip characters frequently portray girls and women as frightened of snakes, frogs, insects, and rats, only to be rescued by the courageous male characters. A recent national television advertisement for a rodent control service depicted a woman descending into her basement with a load of laundry. After she turned on the light, her eyes widened in horror, she dropped the basket of clothing and fled screaming up the stairs, crying out "Bob, Bob, we have rats!" Such media portrayals convey several messages. First, the situation or animal depicted is intrinsically frightening. Second, it is gender specific for females to be terrified upon exposure to such stimuli (and that males will save them). It is clearly established that women come for treatment for simple phobias more frequently than do males (American Psychiatric Association, 1980), and the recent NIMH psychiatric epidemiological study involving home-based structured diagnostic interviews also found the phobic disorders to be more prevalent in women compared to men (Robins et al., 1984).

A small but growing body of experimental evidence is accumulating that supports the hypothesis that a significant percentage of clinical phobias have their origin in exposure to vicarious trauma. The typical procedure is to physiologically monitor an observer while he or she watches another experimental subject (actually a confederate of the researcher) undergo the induction of a miniphobia, obstensibly through being shocked when exposed to certain stimuli such as a specific tone or slide. In reality the confederate only fakes being shocked. After a number of such observational trials it has been shown that the *observer* of this process developes conditioned emotional reactions similar to those of fear, even though he or she never received any shock (Bandura & Rosenthal, 1966; Berger, 1962; Brown, 1974; Craig & Weinstein, 1965). Again, without actually being present when such fears were apparently established during the life history of the clinical phobic, it is impossible to prove that vicarious or observational learning was responsible for the induction of the fear. On balance, however, the evidence seems persuasive.

Psychological Factors. Despite a considerable effort on the part of personality theorists and researchers, no such construct as the "phobic personality" has ever been convincingly demonstrated. Phobics appear to be as diverse in their personality styles and psychological functioning as nonphobics, and it would be a mistake for the human service professional approaching the treatment of a phobic client to impose upon that individual any assumptions pertaining to personality functioning or inherent psychopathology.

Albert Ellis (1973), founder of the popular system known as rational emotive therapy, has maintained that specific phobics represent one major category of anxiety disorders that is reflective of an extremely basic disposition to catastrophize. Such catastrophization is only one of a series of core "irrational" beliefs that Ellis hypothesizes to underlie most emotional disorders. Accordingly, Ellis and other cognitive researchers have attempted to alleviate phobic anxiety through directive therapy aimed at exposing, challenging, and eliminating the irrational beliefs purportedly at the core of the individual's maladaptive responses to anxiety-evoking animals, objects, and situations (Beck and Emery, 1985; Wein, Nelson, & Odom, 1975; Woodward & Jones, 1980). I believe that such efforts may be misguided for most cases of focal phobias. In a correlational study investigating the relationship between adherence to Ellis's irrational beliefs and fears to specific objects, animals, and stimuli, my colleagues and I at the University of Michigan found the relationship to be nil for all intents and purposes, accounting for less than 5% of the variance in Fear Survey scores (Thyer, Papsdorf, & Kramer, 1983). In contrast, adherence to irrational beliefs *has* been shown to correlate quite highly with measures of generalized or nonspecific anxiety (Himle, Thyer, & Papsdorf, 1982; Thyer, Papsdorf, & Kilgore, 1983), suggesting that rational emotive therapy and similar therapeutic approaches may be best targeted to the more pervasive of the anxiety disorders, not to the externally based focal phobias.

Respondent Conditioning. Respondent conditioning is that form of associative learning scientifically investigated for the first time by the Russian physiologist Ivan Pavlov. Most human service professionals are quite familiar with the essential features of his initial studies on reflexive behavior, and how by systematically pairing a neutral stimulus with preexisting or unconditioned stimuli, Pavlov arranged for the neutral stimulus to evoke a response similar to that produced by the unconditioned stimulus. In his prototypical experiment with dogs, after presenting the sound of a bell slightly before the presentation of meat, for a number of trials the sound of the bell alone came to evoke a salivation response. What is not commonly known is that the basic principles of respondent conditioning have been found to be valid with every animal species ever tested, ranging from humans, monkeys, dogs, cats, rats, pigeons, and insects to the snail *Aplysia* (Kandel, 1983) and, at the extreme end of the spectrum, to *single sensory neurons* (Walters & Byrne, 1983)!

The analogy between the principles of respondent conditioning and the phenomenon of acquiring severe phobias via traumatic experience with an animal or situation is compelling. As Ovid noted in *Tristia,* "The least rustle of a feather brings dread upon the dove that thy talons, O hawk, have wounded." Somewhat more empirical observations, again familiar to most human service professionals, were described by Watson and Rayner (1920), who used Pavlovian methods of respondent conditioning to develop a conditioned fear in Little Albert to the sight of a rabbit, a previously neutral stimulus. Indeed, not only would a rabbit cause Albert to burst into tears, but so would other furry objects, such as a Santa Claus mask.

Anecdotally there is much clinical lore to support the hypothesis that some instances of simple and social phobia develop following traumatic exposure to frightening events. Illustrative cases include the 70-year-old woman who became terrified of dogs to such an extent that she practically became housebound, after being viciously attacked by a Saint Bernard (Thyer, 1981). Less violent in origin but still traumatic is the woman who became terrified of frogs after she inadvertently mangled a number of them while cutting her lawn with a power mower (Thyer & Curtis, 1983).

Despite the compelling face validity of such examples, for many years the prevailing view was that most cases of simple and social phobia did *not* have their origins in direct traumatic experiences (Lazarus, 1971; Marks, 1969). In part this perspective was encouraged by studies of analog phobics (e.g., fearful undergraduates), such as that conducted by Rimm, Janda, Lancaster, Nahl, and Dittmar (1977). These researchers, using a volunteer sample of 45 fearful female college students, found only 16 who could give an account of their fears by attributing them to direct traumatic experiences. Such studies and related ones encouraged the notion that respondent conditioning could not account for most instances of phobia onset. What remained unclear was the extent to which such studies employing analog subjects are representative of *clinical* samples of phobic patients, assessed using the DSM-III criteria.

More recent research involving such clinical samples reveals a somewhat different picture. In a sample of 106 phobic patients, Ost and Hugdahl (1981) found that 58% attributed their fears to direct experiences of the conditioning type, a finding upheld by Wolpe (1982), who, using case histories of 40 clinical phobics, found that fully two-thirds of subjects' fears could be accounted for by the processes of respondent conditioning. In a subset of simple phobics, patients with severe fears to blood, illness, or injury (BII phobia), it was found that a large majority (61%) of Ost and Hugdahl's (1985) 73 patients reported the onset of their fears to be associated with direct trauma, and an additional 18% reported vicarious trauma as responsible. In a study with a smaller sample of BII phobics, Thyer, Himle, and Curtis (1985) found that 12 of 15 patients attributed their phobia to either direct (n = 8) or indirect (n = 4) trauma. In their comprehensive review on this subject, Ost and Hugdahl (1985) report, "It seems as if the studies on clinical samples . . . have a higher proportion of patients ascribing the onset of their phobias to conditioning experiences . . . than the studies on analog samples" (p. 28).

It should be noted that in many cases the facts of what are known about phobias are somewhat at variance with the research findings on the processes of respondent conditioning (Costello, 1970; Marks, 1982). A conservative perspective is put forth by Isaac Marks (1981), who recommends that at present human service professionals and researchers avoid the use of labels associated with respondent conditioning in efforts to explain phobic phenomena (i.e., terms such as "conditioned stimulus," "unconditioned stimulus," etc.). Marks suggests that we employ the theory-neutral terms *anxiety-evoking stimulus* (AES) to refer to phobic stimuli (animals, situations, or objects) and *anxiety-evoked response* (AER) to refer to an individual's reactions upon exposure to phobic stimuli. Such terms avoid the implications of a Pavlovian etiology associated with the language of respondent conditioning. The exact relationship between respondent conditioning and the acquisition or maintenance of phobic anxiety undoubtedly will slowly become clearer with additional research.

Positive Reinforcement. The concept of secondary gain (also called *epinosis*) is well known to adherents of psychoanalytic theory and refers to "the obvious advantages that a person gains from his illness, such as gifts, attention, and release from responsibility" (Freedman et al., 1976, p. 1328). This concept is congruent with the process of positive reinforcement known to operant psychologists, referring to the increase in the probability of a behavior when that behavior is followed by the presentation of a reward. In the present analysis operantly oriented human service professionals (as well as their psychodynamic colleagues) should be alert for the possible role that rewards (secondary gain?) may play in the development and maintenance of phobic behavior. Numerous anecdotal case examples may be found in the clinical literature wherein positive reinforcement seems to perpetuate phobic avoidance. The school phobia literature provides some particularly good examples of this process (Ayllon, Smith, & Rogers, 1970; Hersen, 1970; Lazarus, Davison, & Polefka, 1965), with school avoidance clearly being maintained by various positive reinforcers such as extra attention from parents, teachers, siblings, and therapists and by the pleasures of staying home.

The behavioral operation of *shaping*, or of reinforcement of successive approximations, may be relevant here also; the child finding that complaining of stomach aches or other ailments is rewarded by being able to remain home. Increased pressure to attend school may be followed by ever more vehement refusals, protestations, complaints of fears, or somatic disturbances. The periodic times when these tactics "work" and the child remains home renders such behavior ever more difficult to eradicate.

Negative Reinforcement. A related term from the laboratory of the operant psychologist is that of negative reinforcement, referring to the increase in the probability of a behavior when that behavior is followed by the removal of an aversive stimulus. Negative reinforcement also is often invoked as the process responsible for the maintenance of phobic avoidance behavior, often for prolonged periods of time. Take, for example, the dog phobic who is walking down the street, turns a corner, and unexpectedly faces a large German shepherd! Immediately the phobic experiences a surge of terrifying fear. If, as is likely, the person quickly leaves the immediate vicinity of the dog, the act of avoidance is accompanied by gradual reduction in fear. In negative reinforcement language, avoidant behavior (flight) was followed by the removal of an aversive stimulus (the internal sensations of acute fear); thus phobic escape and avoidance is *functional* for the individual, at least in the short term. Over many years the phobic is liable to have experienced many such episodes wherein confrontation with an anxiety-evoking stimulus prompts flight, which helps him or her feel better. In operant terms, such episodes may be construed as learning trials involving negative reinforcement, with each such trial serving to perpetuate the pattern of phobic avoidance.

This formulation of negative reinforcement involving flight followed by relief from phobic anxiety was originally postulated by Mowrer (1939) and continues to be cited as an important mechanism in the *maintenance* (not onset) of simple and social phobias. Actually, Mowrer's theory appears to have some inconsistencies with various technical aspects of respondent and operant conditioning (Herrnstein, 1969; Rachman, 1976); thus uncritical acceptance of the notion that phobic avoidance is maintained by negative reinforcement is un-warranted. As with all theories in an empirical tradition, however, future research will bring with it clarification of this important topic.

SUMMARY

This chapter has reviewed the historical and literary origins of the term *phobia*, along with the contemporary diagnostic criteria for the disorders of simple and social phobia. Descriptive information was presented that outlined demographic and clinical features of these two conditions, and each of the commonly discussed etiological theories was reviewed, along with a discussion of the current status of empirical research supportive or disconfirming of each such theory. Traditional psychodynamic and psychological conceptions of the origins of phobic anxiety have not received as much support as theories relying upon the mechanisms of respondent and operant conditioning and observational learning. Phylogenetic influences undoubtedly play a role in the distribution of certain categories of phobic stimuli. The clinical management of simple and social phobias is described in the following chapter.

Chapter 3

SIMPLE AND SOCIAL PHOBIAS
Treatment Strategies

All fear is painful, and when it conduces not to safety, is painful without use. Every consideration, therefore, by which groundless terrors may be removed, adds something to human happiness.

—Samuel Johnson

Since the beginning of modern theories of psychopathology and the treatment of mental disorders, the construct of anxiety has been a key concept in the understanding of neuroses. Freud's early work with the hysteric "Anna O" and the phobic "Little Hans" eventually led him to the view that the symptomatology of anxiety involved defensive mechanisms designed to keep unacceptable impulses from conscious awareness or from being acted out. From this theory, in part, arose many of the practices of psychoanalysis and psychodynamic psychotherapy. Throughout the development and practice of traditional psychotherapy, however, there has been a somewhat discordant note with respect to the treatment of irrational fears. As noted in Chapter 2, Freud commented that phobic anxiety is *not* accessible to psychotherapy and that mastery of a phobia only occurs when the patient will "go out alone and struggle with the anxiety while they make the attempt [to enter phobic situations]" (Freud, 1894/1955a, pp. 165-166). Other psychodynamic therapists have given similar advice or instructions to their patients, suggesting active confrontation with phobic stimuli either in imagination or in real life (Ferenezi, 1926; Gerz, 1962; Herzberg, 1941; Malleson, 1959; Terhune, 1949).

At one level such suggestions may seem to be little more than applied common sense, as in the advice to get promptly back on the horse that threw you. The German poet Goethe reportedly cured himself of a fear of heights by climbing to the top of the church steeple and remaining

---

AUTHOR'S NOTE: Portions of *Island* by Aldous Huxley are reproduced here by permission of Bantam Books, New York. Copyright © 1962.

there until he calmed down. Over 300 years ago the English philosopher John Locke gave the following advice:

> If your child shrieks and runs away at the sight of a frog let another catch it, and lay it down at a good distance from him; at first accustom him to look upon it; when he can do that, to come nearer to it, and see it leap without emotion; then to touch it lightly, when it is held fast in another's hand; and so on, until he can come to handle it as confidently as a butterfly or a sparrow.

In Aldous Huxley's utopian novel *Island*, the protagonist Will Farnaby is shipwrecked on the tropical island of Pala. In a confused state, Will is severely traumatized by encountering several large snakes, and falls down a cliff. Upon recovering consciousness the following day, he meets Mary Sarojini, a young inhabitant of Pala who cannot understand Will's continued state of terror caused by his memory of the snakes. Perplexed by Will's incapacity, Mary takes charge:

> "Well, if you won't do it for yourself, I'll have to do it for you. Listen Will: there was a snake, a big green snake, and you almost stepped on him. You almost stepped on him, and it gave you such a fright that you lost your balance, you fell. Now say it yourself—say it!"
> "I almost stepped on him," he whispered obediently. "And then I . . ." He couldn't say it. "Then I fell." He brought it out at last, almost inaudibly.
> All the horror of it came back to him—the nausea of fear, the panic start that had made him lose his balance, and then worse fear and the ghastly certainty that it was the end.
> "Say it again."
> "I almost stepped on him. And then . . ."
> He heard himself whimpering.
> "Thats right, Will. Cry—cry!"
> The whimpering became a moaning. Ashamed, he clenched his teeth, and the moaning stopped.
> "No, don't do that," she cried. "Let it come out if it wants to. Remember that snake, Will. Remember how you fell."
> The moaning broke out again and he began to shudder more violently than ever.
> "Now tell me what happened."
> "I could see its eyes, I could see its tongue going in and out."
> "Yes, you could see his tongue. And what happened then?"
> "I lost my balance, I fell."
> "Say it again, Will." He was sobbing now. "Say it again," she insisted.
> "I fell."

"Again."

It was tearing him to pieces, but he said it. "I fell."

"Again, Will." She was implacable. "Again."

"I fell, I fell, I fell . . . "

Gradually the sobbing died down. The words came more easily and the memories they aroused were less painful.

"I fell," he repeated for the hundredth time.

"But you didn't fall very far," Mary Sarojini now said.

"No, I didn't fall very far," he agreed.

"So what's all the fuss about?" the child inquired.

There was no malice or irony in her tone, not the slightest implication of blame. She was just asking a simple straight-forward question that called for a simple straight-forward answer. Yes, what *was* all the fuss about? The snake hadn't bitten him; he hadn't broken his neck. Any anyhow it had all happened yesterday. . . . Will Farnaby laughed aloud. (Huxley, 1962, pp. 12-13)

Clearly the notion that prolonged harmless exposure to phobic stimuli may be of potential therapeutic benefit is not a new one. However, experimental research on the possible benefits of such exposure goes back only to the laboratories of the 1930s and 1940s. At that time researchers would experimentally induce "neurotic" anxiety in laboratory animals in-order to test out various procedures for eliminating such fears. One technique shown to be very useful was called "counterconditioning," or "reciprocal inhibition" (Masserman, 1943; Wolpe, 1952). It was found that an animal fearful of a particular area of a large cage could be induced to overcome such fears by the simple expedient of laying a trail of food from a "safe" area into one that the animal was afraid to enter. Over time the hungry animals crept closer and closer into the "phobic" situation and eventually displayed a complete absence of fear. Control animals, on the other hand, maintained their "experimental neurosis" for prolonged periods. Other attempts were made to relieve experimental neuroses in animals, and alcohol, for one example, was found helpful for this purpose (Masserman & Yum, 1946; Masserman, Jacques, & Nicholson, 1945; Wolpe, 1952).

Such studies led Joseph Wolpe (1958) to develop his theory of reciprocal inhibition as the main basis for psychotherapeutic effects. Wolpe contended that phobic anxiety and other neurotic habits in humans could be successfully overcome by presenting small "doses" of the phobic stimulus to the patient while pairing this exposure with the concurrent presentation of some stimulus whose effects would recipro-cally inhibit the experience of fear. For practical purposes, Wolpe advocated that such exposure should be conducted in the patient's imagination and that the "reciprocal inhibitor" should be the induction of deep muscular relaxation. Treatment thus consisted of thoroughly training the patient in the techniques of progressive muscular relaxation, developing a hierarchy of anxiety-evoking scenes ranging from less to more frightening ones, and then having the patient relax and systematically confront these scenes. If anxiety was inadvertently induced, the patient was instructed to drop the hierarchy scene, reengage the relaxation procedures, and then return in imagination to the hierarchy scene a few moments later when deeply relaxed. In this manner, Wolpe reported that patients could learn to face without fear almost any anxiety-evoking situation that was not realistically harmful. More important, it was claimed that gains obtained via treatment in fantasy transferred quite well to real-life situations. Wolpe (1958) labeled this technique "systematic desensitization."

A number of early uncontrolled group studies supported the efficacy of systematic desensitization. Wolpe (1958) reported that 89% of 210 neurotic patients either apparently recovered completely or were at least 80% improved. Similarly positive results were published by many other researchers. More important, a series of well-controlled group studies also supported the efficacy of systematic desensitization in the treatment of simple and social phobias (Lang & Lazovick, 1963; Lang, Lazovik, & Reynolds, 1965; Paul, 1966). Paul's (1969) review of outcome studies on systematic desensitization found over 20 well-controlled reports and led him to conclude, "For the first time in the history of psychological treatments, a specific therapeutic package reliably produced measurable benefits for clients across a broad range of distressing problems in which anxiety was of fundamental importance."

Following such demonstrations of the efficacy of systematic desensitization in imagination, a number of researchers undertook to isolate the critical ingredients of the treatment package. Puzzlingly, one by one it appeared that none of the supposedly key ingredients of systematic desensitization appeared crucial to a successful outcome, contrary to the underlying theory of the procedure of reciprocal inhibition. Neither relaxation training, hierarchy individualization, nor therapist variables were found to be an essential ingredient, leaving researchers with the puzzling question, "Why does systematic desensitization work?" (Benjamin, Marks, & Huson, 1972; Davis, McLemore, & London; 1970; Emery & Krumboltz, 1967; Ollendick & Nettle, 1977; Rachman, 1968; Sue, 1972).

The answer gradually emerged in a series of studies that examined the relative efficacy of systematic desensitization in imagination conducted with and without real-life homework practice in confronting phobic stimuli. Such studies revealed two very interesting findings: (1) Systematic desensitization conducted exclusively in imagination is decidedly inferior to systematic desensitization conducted with concurrent real-life homework practice (Barlow, Leitenberg, Agras, & Wincze, 1969; Crowe, Marks, Agras, & Leitenberg, 1972; Emmelkamp & Wessels, 1975; Sherman, 1972); and (2) real-life exposure *alone* is an exceptionally effective treatment for phobias in and of itself (Curtis, Nesse, Buxton, Wright, & Lippman, 1976; Barlow & Wolfe, 1981; Greist, Marks, Berlin, Gourney, & Noshiviani, 1980; Linden, 1981; Mathews, 1978). Real-life exposure therapy for the treatment of phobias has also been found to work well with normal children (Ultee, Griffioen, & Schellekens, 1982), mentally retarded adults (Matson, 1981), and the elderly (Thyer, 1981). The status of empirical research at the present time indicates that real-life exposure therapy is the treatment of choice for most clients with simple or social phobias. Table 5 provides a list of the indices and facilitating conditions for the use of therapeutic exposure.

It is important that therapeutic exposure be carried out not only in real life but eventually within the natural contexts of the phobic situations (Thyer, 1985b). After all, most clients are not afraid of *imaginary* snakes, dogs, bridges, or public speaking occasions but of their real-life counterparts. Accordingly, treatment conducted in real-life contexts is far more likely to result in real-life improvements than treatment conducted in the client's imagination. As a general rule, therapeutic exposure to anxiety-evoking stimuli in *fantasy* is primarily indicated if it is not possible to reproduce in real life the client's fears, or if time constraints preclude arranging real-life sessions (e.g., an imminent airplane trip). Other clinical examples here could include phobias to such stimuli as thunderstorms, lightning, speeches before large public gatherings, professional musical performances, or transatlantic flight.

TREATMENT STRATEGY

During the initial evaluation session the human service professional should ensure that the client meets the prerequisites for exposure therapy listed in Table 5. Time should be spent engaging the client in a therapeutic alliance characterized by the usual conditions associated with all good clinical practice, such as empathy, warmth, and genuineness. It is often helpful to have on hand a number of self-help books for

Table 5:   Indications for the Use of Exposure Therapy

1. The client meets the DMS-III criteria for simple or social phobia (see table 1).
2. The client is committed to working hard to overcome his or her fears.
3. It is possible for the human service professional to arrange to reproduce the essential aspects of the client's anxiety-evoking stimulus.
4. The human service professional and client can jointly plan a projected program of graduated exposure to the anxiety-evoking stimuli, working from less to more frightening situations.
5. The client is willing, with or without a support person, to confront anxiety-evoking stimuli and to maintain this contact until anxiety subsides.

the treatment of phobias which the client may borrow or purchase. The best of these is *Living with Fear* by Isaac Marks (1974), although there are others (Melville, 1977; Smith, 1977; Zane & Milt, 1984; Zimbardo, 1977) which you may find useful. Such books serve several purposes. First, they provide reassurance to the client, above and beyond your own efforts, that they are not alone in suffering from "crazy" or irrational fears. Second, they contain numerous examples of individuals who successfully overcame similar fears, providing the client with positive expectancies. Third, such books go into greater detail on the rationale for real-life exposure therapy than the human service professional with a heavy caseload may have time to explain. Such books should *not* be construed as an adequate substitute for a thorough review and discussion of therapeutic exposure with a client, but as an adjunct they give the client something tangible to consult when needed. Fourth, clients can share the information and case histories in these self-help books with their long-suffering spouses, family, or friends, saying in effect, "See, I'm not the only one with this problem and since these people overcame it, with your help I can too."

Next, the human service professional engages the client in the process of *stimulus mapping*, isolating the critical ingredients of the client's unique anxiety-evoking stimuli. This is necessary to plan the actual steps of therapeutic exposure. People are individuals, and not all phobics are alike. One dog phobic may be terrified of being bitten, whereas another abhors the sensation of being licked, while yet a third shudders at the sound of a dog's bark. Some spider phobics tolerate quite well the sight of a spider on the floor but go into paroxysms of terror if one is crawling above their head on the wall. The so-called speech phobic may be found to be quite calm when addressing children or inferiors at work; another does best with large audiences, not small, intimate ones. A height phobic may enjoy the view from a small window on the fifth floor yet be reduced to a mass of tremors when on the fifth story of an open parking structure.

It can be seen that each patient needs to be approached as an individual, without preconceived notions on the part of the clinician as to how treatment should proceed. The initial steps of stimulus mapping may be conducted in the office, relying on the client's responses to questions asked by the inquiring human service professional. Ask clients if there are any circumstances wherein they are *not* afraid, or less fearful, of their anxiety-evoking stimulus; likewise probe for those situations in which fearfulness is at its peak. Through a series of skillful questions the human service professional can eventually construct, in writing, a hierarchy of graduated tasks or circumstances involving potential exposure to the client's anxiety-evoking stimulus. You should review this with the client to be sure that you have a clear understanding of the specific things of which the client is afraid, and then rank them in correct order of their fear-evoking potential.

The next step is for the human service professional and the client to mutually agree where on this list of phobic stimuli treatment should begin. Traditional systematic desensitization began with the lowest item on the client's hierarchy of fear-evoking cues. In real-life therapeutic exposure it is best to allow clients to make this choice, suggesting that they try to challenge themselves moderately at the onset of treatment. It would not be good practice for the clinician to say, "Alright Mr. Jones, we will begin next week with the adult German shepherd dog. Be here in my office at your usual time." Your caseload would likely become quite small very quickly! Clients should never be forced to approach or encounter phobic stimuli at a rate faster than they give their consent to. Note, however, that clients need *not* be comfortable and relaxed, only that they give their consent for a greater level of approach. It is not atypicial for a well-motivated client, with tears streaming down his or her face, to move resolutely closer to a frightening animal. In fact, the more anxiety they are willing to tolerate during treatment sessions the faster clients will overcome their phobia. Tedious plodding through a hierarchy of phobic stimuli, either in fantasy or imagination, with minimal anxiety *will* eventually produce a satisfactory result in that the client's fears will dissipate, but the financial cost to the client will be correspondingly greater, not to mention the cost in time and energy. Clinician factors also suggest that treatment should progress as rapidly as the client will allow. Certainly sessions are much more interesting for all parties concerned! Another consideration is service connected. The clinician who treats one client with very slow therapeutic exposure, perhaps taking 50 hours, will have a satisfied client, but assuming that a more aggressive approach would have resolved the phobia in 10 hours, that professional will have in effect denied treatment to four other people on the agency's waiting list. Human service professionals in private practice are under no such constraint, but professional ethics dictate that one retain a client in therapy only to the extent that this is therapeutically justifiable.

You should proceed in a stepwise manner in order to arrive at an agreement as to where to begin with the first treatment session. The following dialogue is reconstructed from a preliminary session with a severely snake phobic woman:

> Therapist: Would you be willing to begin next week by looking at a caged foot-long snake from 15 feet away?
>
> Client: NO! [emphatically]
>
> Therapist: How about from 30 feet away?
>
> Client: No! I don't want to look at any snakes.
>
> Therapist: Would you be willing to look at a toy rubber snake from 15 feet away?
>
> Client: No! No rubber snakes either.
>
> Therapist: Alright, how about a small photograph of a snake? [from my collection]
>
> Client: No, I can't stand to look at pictures of snakes either. I make my husband cut them out of our magazines before I read them.
>
> Therapist: O.K., would you be able to look at realistic drawing of a snake?
>
> Client: No, I don't think so. That would be too difficult a place to begin for me.
>
> Therapist: How about if we used a cartoon of a snake, one from the Sunday comic strips? [from my collection]
>
> Client: No, that would be too frightening too.
>
> Therapist: Suppose I covered up the cartoon of the snake with a piece of cardboard, so that you can see only one-eighth of an inch of the tip of the cartoon snake's tail? I could cover it up altogether if you then asked me to.
>
> Client: Welllll. . . . I suppose I could try that, but only if you promise me not to make me look at the whole thing all at once.

Bingo. That is where we began treatment. After prolonged exposure to increasing bits of the cartoon, we moved to drawings of snakes, photos, nature movies of snakes, at first greatly blurred and then brought in focus, toy snakes, and then the real things borrowed from a cooperative pet store. At the end of 12 sessions she was comfortably catching live snakes I had placed in the grass for her to find.

There are a number of self-report inventories that can facilitate the process of stimulus mapping. Wolpe and Lang (1977) have prepared the *Fear Survey Schedule,* which is one of the more comprehensive of such instruments, listing 108 potential anxiety-evoking stimuli. Clients are asked to rate how fearful they are of each listed object, animal, or situation. Normative data for the Fear Survey Schedule based upon patients with DSM-III-defined anxiety disorders are available (Tomlin, Thyer, Curtis, Nesse, Cameron, & Wright, 1984), and the instrument appears to be free of gender biases (Thyer, Tomlin, Curtis, Cameron, & Nesse, 1985). A version suitable for use with children is also available (Ollendick, 1983).

The one-page Fear Questionnaire by Marks and Mathews (1979) is also a useful instrument for stimulus-mapping purposes, providing not only a simple measure of how much a person is *afraid* of potential anxiety-evoking stimuli but also how much actual phobic *avoidance* behavior these fears engender.

Raulin and Wee (1984) have recently published a useful Social Fear Scale consisting of 44 true/false questions pertaining to the aversiveness of various social situations. Like the Fear Survey Schedule, the Social Fear Scale may be used for stimulus mapping. If possible, clients should complete these measures and return them to you prior to your first appointment with them. These instruments should not be viewed as either psychological "tests" or as diagnostic tools but rather as assessment aids to help the human service professional save a little time in attempting to get a clear and accurate picture of the parameters of the client's phobia. They are not to be used as substitutes for careful one-on-one evaluative interviewing but as useful adjuncts.

Obviously, clients may be somewhat dubious at embarking on a course of therapeutic exposure. The following reassurances are often helpful:

(1) There will be no tricks or surprises. I will always ask and obtain your permission prior to introducing a new level of exposure.

(2) At any time, you may ask me to temporarily remove the anxiety-evoking stimulus (or for us to leave the situation). I *will do so immediately* upon your firm request.

(3) You can terminate our session at any time you wish.

After giving these reassurances, point out to clients that in actuality *they* will have full control of the treatment session and that they do not have to do anything they do not wish to attempt. At this point, most clients will be willing to try at least one session with you, and it is crucial that if they "test" you—for example, by asking you to remove the anxiety-evoking stimulus temporarily—that you promptly abide by their request. After a few such tests the resultant sense of control over the situation the client experiences goes a long way toward quelling any doubts they may have as to your trustworthiness.

Here are two other points to take into account when planning the initial treatment sessions. First, *long sessions are better than short ones.* By "long" I mean sessions on the order of two or more hours. It has been experimentally shown that two consecutive hours of therapeutic exposure produce significantly greater clinical benefits than four half-hour separated sessions (Stern & Marks, 1973). As a general rule, one makes more progress the longer one engages in prolonged exposure; hence clients obtain a greater sense of progress and satisfaction after a prolonged session than a short one. This usually enhances motivation to continue in treatment because improvements are often quite marked from session to session.

Second, if therapeutic exposure is to be of benefit, *marked improvements are usually noted during and after the first few sessions.* Thus the skeptical client is quickly won over. There are few things the phobic finds as satisfying as comfortably encountering an animal, object, or situation that filled him or her with dread only a session or so ago. Alternatively, if little progress is evident after several sessions of exposure, this is a sign for the clinician to consider alternative treatment options or to review the stimulus-mapping procedure.

Below are some case histories describing the conduct of therapeutic exposure in representative cases of simple and social phobia.

CASE 1: FEAR OF ENCLOSED PLACES

Donald was a 33-year-old single man who came to the Anxiety Disorders Program and requested help in overcoming his fear of enclosed places. He worked as a computer repairman and was often called to large office buildings or skyscrapers to perform his repairs. Rather than ride the elevators, Donald would struggle up the stairwell carrying his heavy tool kit, often for several dozen stories. Socially he was impaired in that on dates he could not go to certain restaurants atop tall buildings. He found that his dates balked at the idea of trudging up the stairs in high heels when there was a perfectly good elevator at hand. Several times when he had completed his repairs, an office acquaintance would suggest that they go out to lunch. This too presented cause for embarrassment when the person would find Donald opting for the stairs to descend the building. A secret fear of Donald's was that someday he would be arrested and placed in jail. He was convinced he would go berserk in an attempt to prevent himself from being placed in a small jail cell, or driven insane by the confinement. Donald also reported severe fears to traveling by buses, trains, or airplanes. The onset of his fear was not possible to trace; Donald reported being afraid of enclosed places all his life. He met the DSM-III criteria for simple phobia but for no other mental disorder.

The initial agreed-upon treatment approach was a variety of exposure therapy involving reinforced practice of successive approximations. A small, well-lighted room approximately 5 by 5 feet square was used for the first few treatment sessions. This room could be locked from the outside so that anyone inside could not escape until released by someone else. Donald agreed, with some trepidation, to allow me to lock him in the room for a brief period of time. He was to sit in a comfortable chair and carefully watch a portable heart rate monitor I gave him. (Such instruments can be inexpensively purchased at most sporting goods stores.) Heart rate was to be used as one measure of Donald's fearful reactions to confinement.

The second measure was his self-report of anxiety, quantified in the form of Wolpe's (1969) Subjective Anxiety Scale. This simply involves asking the client to construct an imaginary scale ranging from 0, representing a state of complete relaxation, to 100, representing the most fear ever experienced. This is an easy way to quantify a client's subjective reactions during the conduct of therapeutic exposure, and most individuals pick up the use of the scale very quickly. Despite its apparent simplicity, the Subjective Anxiety Scale has been shown to correlate reasonably well with heart rate and skin temperature, two commonly used indices of autonomic arousal (Thyer, Papsdorf, Davis, & Vallecorsa, 1984).

The third index of fear was the time spent in the room, specifically the duration of time Donald was willing to undergo on each trial. Treatment proceeded as follows. Donald was asked to pick a time period during which he would be willing to be locked in the room. I told him I would remain outside the door but I would not release him until the agreed time period had elapsed. Obviously this was a difficult challenge, but Donald agreed to give it a try—but only for 30 seconds the first trial. His further instructions were to note the highest heart rate that appeared on the pulse monitor during this 30-second interval, as well as the highest level of subjective anxiety he experienced. With lavish praise to him, I closed the door, carefully timed a 30-second interval, and then opened the door to reveal a white-faced Donald still in his chair. He told me that his highest heart rate was 128 beats per minute and his subjective anxiety peaked at 80 (in other words, he was 80% as frightened as he had ever been in his life). I again praised him lavishly and asked him if he was willing to attempt the experience again. He agreed, but only for another 30-second period. The process was repeated a second trial, and then a third, and so on. The entire session lasted 1½ hours and involved a total of 14 trials of remaining in the locked room for longer periods of time. The data for this first treatment session are displayed in Figure 3.

As can be seen, Donald's anxiety declined over the course of the session from 80% to 20%, despite the fact that he increased his length of time in the room from 30 seconds to 10 minutes. Inspection of his heart rate data also revealed modest decreases over the length of the treatment session, supportive of his self-reports of decreased fear. It was interesting to watch his changes in mood over the course of the session. Initially he was tremulous and apprehensive but with each consecutive successful trial he grew more and more self-confident. Toward the end he was flashing me a big smile when I opened the door at the expiration of the agreed time period, and commenting on how easy it had become. I used lots of appropriate praise and encouragement for him to try longer periods of time. The data in Figure 3 are typical of the magnitude of improvements seen in the initial sessions of therapeutic exposure, and Donald's positive experiences in overcoming his fear increased his commitment to continuing with me.

Future sessions consisted of more of the same, gradually increasing the length of time Donald was spending in the room to a half hour. At this point I suggested that we increase the difficulty of the exposure by having me leave the proximity of the room Donald was waiting in. I thought that by having me outside the door, Donald may have derived some comfort from the thought that I would release him if he yelled to get out. He agreed that this would indeed be more difficult but agreed to try it. Initally he regressed somewhat in that he stipulated that he remain in the room only for a one-minute interval while I was gone. I agreed to this, of course, and after the first few trials Donald found that nothing untoward happened, enabling him to quickly increase the duration he remained in the room to 30 minutes.

I now suggested a more difficult exposure task, that of remaining in the locked room, without anyone nearby, *in the dark*. Again Donald agreed but stipulated a one-minute interval for the first trial of this new, more difficult task. With little difficulty he habituated to this situation, remaining comfortably in the dark room without anyone within earshot

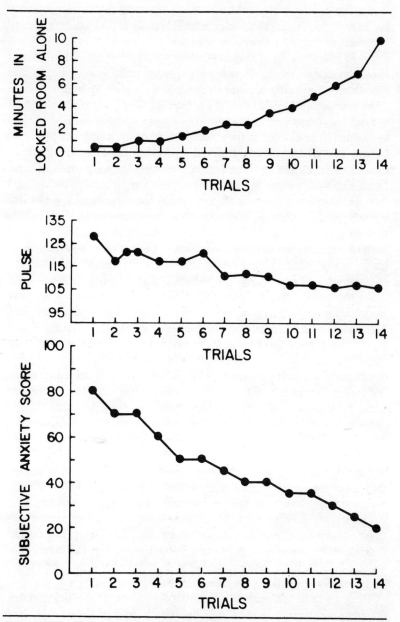

Figure 3. The effects of one session of reinforced practice for a claustrophobic male (Case 1).

for 30 minutes. He felt this was remarkable progress considering that we had met for only five treatment sessions.

I now felt it was time to begin practice within more natural contexts. I chose a rickety freight elevator in an older building on campus and scheduled an evening appointment when we would be undisturbed. I demonstrated to Donald that if I permitted the elevator door to close behind me, there was no mechanism for me to open the door unless someone either opened it from the outside or the occupant pressed a button for another floor. Proceeding as before, Donald agreed to remain in the closed elevator for progressively longer periods of time. Desensitization proceeded quickly without any untoward incidents. I then suggested we progress to my leaving the vicinity of the elevator while he remained inside, and we eventually unscrewed the lightbulb in the elevator so that at the conclusion of therapy Donald was in a pitch dark elevator for upwards of 30 minutes. I introduced a variable time frame as well, in that rather than giving him a set interval "I will be back in 15 minutes," I was saying, "I'll be back sometime within half an hour."

At this point I had begun asking Donald to try real-life homework assignments involving elevators. Initially these were of minimal demand, such as to board an elevator on the ground floor and ride it to the second floor. He was to do this repeatedly until it got boring and then ride to the third floor, and so on. Treatment thus moved from my structuring and conducting exposure therapy sessions with Donald to more of an instigative approach, wherein he would agree to attempt certain homework assignments during the week between appointments and then come to discuss them with me, covering the points of difficulty and of success. Once one assignment was confidently behind him, we would jointly plan the next exposure task. Eventually I faded out the weekly one-on-one sessions and substituted contacts by phone. At the conclusion of treatment Donald was comfortably riding elevators for any necessary length of time, and periodically made a point of riding them even if it was not necessary as a form of booster session. Concurrent with these behavioral improvements, Donald's social limitations and embarrassing experiences in daily living became unpleasant and even somewhat laughable past memories. As might be expected, his self-esteem and confidence generally improved as well.

Perhaps I was fortunate that he never did "panic" in the locked room. By very cautiously increasing the length of time, however, and progressing relatively slowly, I hedged my bets against that happening. If I had structured treatment so that we *began* in an old unlit elevator, I doubt that Donald would have complied. Certainly the degree of input he had into the conduct of treatment immensely increased his confidence and trust in me. The real-life homework was a crucial aspect in ensuring that the improvements generated in formal treatment generalized and maintained in Donald's real life. Further, the gradual fade-out regarding my own involvement also facilitated this process. At the end the client was literally conducting his own treatment and possessed the knowledge and resources to cope with any tendencies toward relapse. My total commitment to the case was about 10 sessions, involving 17 hours of my time.

CASE 2: FEAR OF FROGS

Linda was a 27-year-old married woman who referred herself to the Anxiety Disorders Program due to a debilitating fear of frogs. The traumatic onset of this fear occurred three years earlier when she had accidently run a power lawnmower over what appeared to be a nest of frogs in the backyard of her rural home. She was sprayed with bits of mutilated frogs and surrounded by dozens of the animals trying to escape. Her home was on a riverbank and she frequently encountered frogs in her yard, once actually having to flee her home when one hopped into her kitchen through the back door. The evenings were a torment for Linda as she was forced to listen to a nightly chorus of bellowing frogs that lived on the riverbank. She suffered from frequent nightmares about frogs and related insomnia, and met the DSM-III criteria for a simple phobia.

Treatment options were presented to Linda, who elected to pursue real-life exposure therapy, and in this instance standardized behavioral approach tests were used to quantify phobic anxiety before and after each treatment session. The behavioral approach test consists of the therapist gradually approaching the seated client while carrying or holding the phobic object or animal, halting at specified increments of distance, and obtaining client permission prior to approaching closer. At each standardized increment of distance, the client's subjective anxiety is measured using Wolpe's Subjective Anxiety Scale (0 = completely calm, 100 = panic-stricken). In addition, I employed the portable heart rate monitor to measure the client's pulse during the behavioral approach test. As is previously discussed with the client, the therapist stops approaching when the client instructs him or her to come no further and when that maximum approach has been achieved. This behavioral approach test procedure requires only a few minutes to conduct and enables the clinician to assess objectively the magnitude of the client's phobic disorder through concurrent measures of avoidance behavior (how close the client permits the anxiety-evoking stimulus), subjective anxiety (Wolpe's scale), and physiological arousal (heart rate).

The data for the pre- and posttreatment behavioral approach tests for the first treatment session are presented in Figure 4. The rightmost datapoint represents the maximum level of approach that Linda permitted during that assessment. The varying increments of distance are noted on the horizontal axis (OR = out of room; 15 feet through 1 foot represent distances from the client; IT = indirectly touching the phobic animal by touching the container; DT = directly touching the phobic animal; HOLD = holding the phobic animal; UC = allowing unlimited contact with the phobic animal). Linda's subjective anxiety scores (maximum = 100) and heart rate are denoted on the vertical axis. As can be seen in Figure 4, pretreatment Linda was able to permit the therapist holding a frog to come within 6 feet of her, gave a subjective anxiety rating of 65% at this point, and had marked tachycardia (racing pulse). After one and a half hours of exposure therapy the behavioral approach test was conducted in an identical manner, and marked improvements can be seen. Both subjective anxiety and heart rate were decreased and significantly closer approach was permitted.

This pattern of assessing the client's phobia pre and post each treatment session was continued and the data for sessions three and six (the final one) are presented in Figures 5 and 6. As can be seen, the exposure therapy appeared to produce successive and substantial decrements in phobic anxiety, and at the end of treatment Linda was free of all functional limitations due to her fear of frogs and able to encounter them without apprehension. Nightmares and insomnia were also alleviated. It should be noted that treatment took place outside the office during the latter sessions, in lawns and meadows, with the client catching freely hopping frogs. I was able to borrow frogs without charge from a biology laboratory located nearby. The next case history describes the treatment of a severely social phobic man.

CASE 3: SOCIAL PHOBIA

This 56-year-old male autoworker, Fred, was also self-referred to the Anxiety Disorders Program, and his presenting complaints were of extreme apprehension, fears of fainting, marked tremor, and agitation, which were reliably evoked whenever he was in situations involving face-to-face interactions with someone else. This was impairing his ability to work and had greatly restricted his social life. In addition he could not stand in lines with people or attend communion at his church. Mild depression was a sequelae of these restrictions, and when I

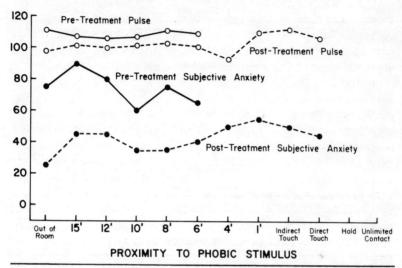

Figure 4. Pre- and posttreatment behavioral approach tests for the first exposure therapy session for a simple phobic (Case 2).

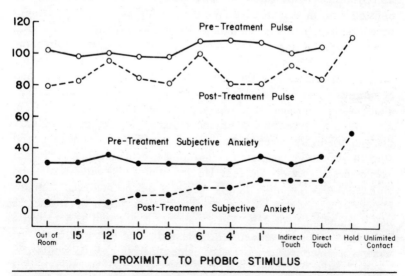

Figure 5. Pre- and posttreatment behavioral approach tests for the third exposure therapy session for a simple phobic (Case 2).

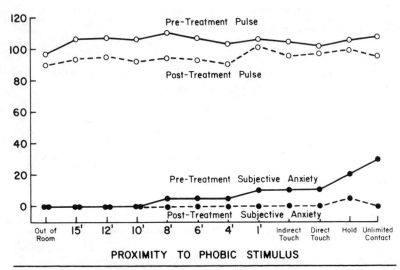

Figure 6. Pre- and posttreatment behavioral approach tests for the sixth (final) exposure therapy session for a simple phobic (Case 2).

evaluated him Fred met the diagnostic criteria for social phobia. He dated the onset of his fears to an episode 30 years earlier when he was an enlisted man in the military. While standing at attention during a morning role call, his commanding officer abruptly came up, stood in front of him, and verbally abused him for several minutes in front of the other troops. It was, it turned out, a case of mistaken identity—the officer had erroneously thought that Fred was a soldier who had committed some infraction when in reality it was someone else. The client was proscribed from replying to the officer's abuse or from attempting to correct his commander due to the dictates of military discipline. This was an exceedingly embarrassing episode for Fred, and since that event similar situations had come to evoke identical feelings of helplessness, agitation, and fear. He was comfortable with his wife and children and a few other family members but no one else. Stimulus mapping revealed that his fearful reactions were at their worst when he had to stand *unsupported.* When seated or if he could lean against a wall, Fred was relatively comfortable and could converse freely. At work if a supervisor or coworker came up to talk, Fred would rest against the work table. If completely alone—in the woods, for example—Fred was at his most relaxed and wandered freely.

Employing a learning theory perspective, I hypothesized that Fred's social phobia was an example of a classically conditioned emotional response. The process of stimulus generalization caused the fear to spread to other situations bearing features resembling the original traumatic episode. Fred agreed to undertake exposure therapy with me, and, being clearly willing to tolerate a good deal of anxiety, opted for a fairly tough first task. I asked Fred to stand unsupported in the middle of my office (I had pushed the furniture against the walls) and with his consent I stood directly in front of him with my eyes about 10 inches from his. At the beginning of this stance I asked Fred to give me a rating of his anxiety, using the subjective anxiety scale I had previously described to him. I jotted down the number and continued to stare at him. Similar measures of Fred's anxiety were obtained at two-minute intervals over the next 20 minutes.

The results were quite dramatic. Within a few minutes Fred had developed a marked tremor, broke out in profuse perspiration on his brow, and made several abortive efforts to reach out to a chair for support. With much verbal reassurance and encouragement Fred was able to remain standing in this position, and, much to his surprise, he began to calm down after about 10 minutes had elapsed. The tremor grew less marked and was absent after about 15 minutes. At the end of the 20-minute session the client's anxiety was back down to its original, relatively low level (20%). Fred was exceedingly pleased, exclaiming "I can't believe it, here I am standing in front of you and I am completely relaxed! I haven't been able to do this in 30 years!"

In point of fact Fred had never tried to tolerate his social anxiety in this manner. Like most phobics, he had made elaborate arrangements in his life to avoid precisely this type of situation involving prolonged confrontation with anxiety-evoking stimuli. On those occasions when he did find himself face to face with someone else, he fled the situation as soon as possible, usually with an excuse such as needing to find the bathroom or an unfinished task. The data from the first three sessions of exposure therapy in Fred's treatment are presented in Figure 7 and demonstrate the improvements made in the client's becoming comfortable in the situation described above. Although his anxiety peaked at 60% of panic during the first treatment session, it never again reached that level in subsequent sessions. Sessions two and three were conducted in an identical manner to that described above, devoted to Fred's becoming desensitized to standing in front of me while unsupported. Both his subjective anxiety and overt fearfulness grew progressively less severe and decreased more rapidly each session.

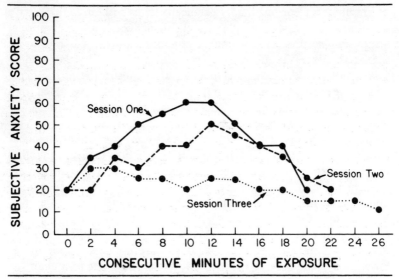

Figure 7. The effects of three sessions of exposure therapy on subjective anxiety in a social phobic (Case 3).

Following these successful office sessions, which greatly improved Fred's confidence that he would overcome his fears, I suggested we move to more real-life settings. We agreed to meet at a local movie theater on "Dollar Night" when lines were sure to be long. Indeed, this was the case; the queue stretched around the block. Fred and I stood side by side as I carefully monitored his reactions and made sure he did not lean against the wall for support. When we got to the front of the line, we stepped out of the queue and unobtrusively rejoined it at the end. This session also went well and was followed by others at fast food restaurants during the busy lunch hour and at cafeterias.

At one point while standing in line I asked Fred what his greatest fear was at that moment. He replied he feared having people see his hands shaking. (He was actually quite calm at this point without any tremulousness.) I asked what he thought might happen, and he indicated that they would point and laugh at him. I said, "Alright, Fred, I'm going to pretend I have a tremor in my right hand and I would like for you to carefully watch the others and observe their reactions. Are you willing to do that?" He agreed, and I proceeded to demonstrate a Parkinson's-like tremor as we continued to converse and wait in the extended line. After five minutes I asked him to report on what he observed, and he quite correctly pointed out that I was pretty much ignored and that the few people who looked at me quickly glanced away.

I then asked him to demonstrate an intentional tremor and with some verbal persuasion he eventually did so. To his amazement he too was ignored by the crowd, even when, at my request, he stopped trembling in his right arm and began a tremor in his left in an attempt deliberately to call attention to himself and his peculiar actions. This strategy could be interpreted as a paradoxical technique, in that by asking him to re-create in real life his greatest fear he found that nothing untoward happened, effectively pricking the balloon of anxiety he had hovering over him for 30 years.

We then began the gradual shift from accompanied sessions to more self-conducted treatment and homework assignments. He attended communion at church on Sunday by waiting until the communion line was almost terminated and then quietly joining it. The following week he waited until it was halfway finished and then joined the line, and so forth. He accepted invitations to social gatherings such as weddings (events he had previously avoided), standing in receiving lines and waiting in buffet queues. Treatment involved eight sessions, and a three-year follow-up found that these gains had been maintained. His wife stated that he was like an entirely different person, having joined a bowling league, and was now taking her out in a whirlwind of social activities.

SPECIAL PROBLEMS

Like all clinical interventions, the conduct of therapeutic exposure often entails special problems. The specific indications for the use of exposure therapy were listed in Table 5, but it is important for the human service professional to be aware of those factors, listed in Table 6, that *contraindicate* the use of these procedures.

In the event that some physical disorder precludes the induction of severe fear, the therapist should turn to the less anxiety-evoking procedures, such as very slow real-life exposure or systematic desensitization in imagination. If the physical disorder is likely to be of short duration (e.g., a healing stomach ulcer) and the client's phobia is of such limited impact that treatment may be considered "elective," the client and therapist may mutually agree to delay therapy for several months.

For obvious reasons of noncompliance, the paranoid or acutely psychotic individual is not likely to be amenable to a suggested course of exposure therapy. Less anxiety-evoking procedures such as systematic desensitization in imagination have been successfully employed in the treatment of chronic schizophrenics who also had simple phobias, however (Himle & Shorkey, 1973; Shorkey & Himle, 1974).

Table 6:   Contraindications for the Use of Exposure Therapy

1. The client has a physical condition that precludes the induction of severe anxiety (e.g., ulcerative colitis, cardiovascular disease, asthma, etc.).
2. The client suffers from paranoid disorder or is acutely psychotic.
3. The client is addicted to or abusive of alcohol or drugs.
4. The client is severely depressed.

In the event that the client has come to abuse alcohol or sedative drugs in an attempt to cope with phobic anxiety, Marks (1985) suggests that a precursor to exposure therapy is that the client reduce alcohol intake to 1.5 ounces of pure alcohol, 7.5 mg of diazepam (Valium), or their equivalents. Such alcohol or drug use is a form of escape or avoidance behavior that must be reduced if exposure therapy is to be of maximum benefit. Severe alcohol or drug addiction must be treated in its own right.

Severely depressed anxious patients do not respond well to exposure therapy, probably due to a failure to habituate to the anxiety-evoking stimulus within treatment sessions (Foa, 1979; Foa et al., 1983). In such cases a pre-exposure therapy course of antidepressant drugs may prove useful, or a course of psychosocial therapy designed to reduce depression.

Exposure therapy has been shown to be as acceptable to clients as is traditional psychotherapeutic approaches to treatment (Marks, 1981), and the client dropout rate is generally low due to the early positive results obtained with most clients. Approximately 5% of clients fail to experience anxiety reduction with prolonged exposure to anxiety-evoking stimuli, however. The precise reasons for this are not known. In such cases the human service professional should carefully review the possibilities for a differential diagnosis (Cameron, 1985) and the stimulus-mapping procedure to be sure that the critical features of the client's anxiety-evoking stimuli have been accurately determined.

During exposure therapy clients may engage in a variety of overt and covert avoidant responses designed to distract themselves or otherwise reduce anxiety. Such avoidance behaviors may effectively preclude complete habituation during the course of treatment, and the human service professional needs to be alert for such activities. Clients may carry or wear certain apparel (e.g., sunglasses, hats, umbrellas, canes, large purses) designed to "protect" themselves from the anxiety-evoking stimulus. Partial turning away or closing of the eyes are equivalent operations. Such behaviors may be permitted in the early stages of treatment, but eventually the human service professional should instruct or coax the client to give them up.

Very rarely, clients report unusual sensory experiences during an exposure therapy session, possibly related to the induction of severe anxiety (Curtis, 1981). Examples are the spider phobic who, upon observing a spider in a jar, reports the tactile sensation of a spider crawling on his or her arm. Clients have also reported paresthesias and vertigo-like reactions. Feelings of mild depersonalization may also occur during a session. There are no good explanations for any of these phenomena, which are always transient, harmless, and unrelated to treatment outcomes. In the early stages of therapeutic exposure, some clients complain of restless sleep or of nightmares the evening before or after a treatment session. These reactions also pass in time.

Adherence to mutually agreed-upon self-exposure homework assignments can be enhanced through several strategies. The first is giving the client a thorough grounding in the rationale for therapeutic exposure and to stress that treatment benefits accrue in direct proportion to the amount of time he or she engages in prolonged exposure to anxiety-evoking stimuli. If this is attended to for only two hours a week, accompanied by the human service professional, clients will eventually overcome their phobias, albeit slowly. However, if they practice for 10 hours a week, two with you and eight alone or with a support person, they will overcome their fears five times as fast. Second, initially suggest as homework assignments activities you and the client have successfully practiced together, rather than expecting him or her to undertake new and greater challenges alone. Of course, in the latter stages of treatment a greater degree of autonomy in self-exposure practice should be encouraged. Third, it is often helpful to have the clients keep a diary or log of their homework practice, recording when and where they practiced and how they coped. Subjective anxiety ratings may also be recorded on these logs, which should be brought into the next appointment with the human service professional, where they document client assertions of practice and serve as a focus of discussion and as a guide to choosing the next week's activities. Fourth, noncompliance with agreed-upon homework tasks, thus retarding progress, may be due to imposing on clients assignments that are too challenging. In such instances simply arrange to have them attempt less frightening self-exposure tasks.

Rarely one may see a client who fails to cooperate due to reasons of secondary gain. In such instances phobic behavior may be intentionally or inadvertently reinforced via some external contingency. For example, phobic and dependent behavior may serve as a mechanism to obtain spousal attention, or a client may be receiving a disability pension due to his/her fears. If the former situation does not respond to your counseling, referral to a marital or family therapist may be indicated. As an example of the latter case, I saw a client who had been employed as a butcher in a large supermarket. He developed a severe blood phobia after being accidentally shot, and, unable to return to work, was receiving a 100% psychiatric disability pension. Such cases are exceedingly difficult to treat successfully, and despite the best apparent efforts of such patients, failure or relapse is common.

Occasionally the adjunctive use of antianxiety medications may be helpful for the client who apparently fails to experience any reduction in anxiety during prolonged exposure. In such cases a moderate dosage of one of the benzodiazapines may be given *prior to* an exposure therapy session. Try to structure such medication use so that the client is experiencing peak antianxiety effects when therapeutic exposure *begins*, so that the drug's effects are waning during the course of the session (Johnston & Gath, 1973). In our clinic we have found that 1 mg of alprazolam (Xanax) given two hours before a session is helpful in this regard. For clients with a pronounced somatic component to their anxiety reaction, particularly cardiovascular symptoms, a beta-blockading agent such as 40 mg of propranolol (Inderal) may be employed instead of the benzodiazapine compounds (Noyes, 1982). Over time this use of adjunctive medications should be faded out and standard techniques of therapeutic exposure pursued.

Human service professionals planning to employ exposure therapy in their practice need to be psychologically prepared for the client who becomes greatly upset. Not only do you need to employ appropriate reassurance, support, and encouragement, but you must come to terms with your own role as an individual who is directly responsible for a client's extreme distress. Such a role is by no means unique to practitioners of exposure therapy. Psychoanalysts use cathartic techniques, alcohol counselors employ family confrontation tactics, and client-centered therapists frequently have their clients weeping. Such therapeutic tools have the same goals as exposure therapy, promoting the long-term mental health of the client. Just as our clients come to be less afraid of the dog or snake, the human service professional using exposure therapy techniques learns that client responses of tearfulness and agitation are a part of the therapeutic process and, while prepared to empathize, is at the same time able to continue the session as the client permits. The therapist's rewards come at the end of treatment when the client is no longer dominated by irrational fears and the positive changes your clients have made can be seen clearly.

Chapter 4

AGORAPHOBIA AND PANIC DISORDER
Diagnosis, Etiology, and Assessment

"Then comes my fit again: I had else been perfect,
Whole as the marble, founded as the rock,
As broad and general as the casing air:
But now I am cabin'd, cribb'd, confined,
Bound in to saucy doubts and fears.'

—Shakespeare, *Macbeth*

With the advent of the DSM-III in 1980, the well-known diagnosis of agoraphobia was listed as a subcategory of the so-called phobic disorders, together with simple and social phobia. A refinement of the newer diagnostic nomenclature was to denote two varieties of agoraphobia: agoraphobia with panic attacks and agoraphobia without panic attacks. Relatively unambiguous diagnostic criteria were listed for these diagnoses (see Table 7), and clinically such clients are easy to recognize given the severe functional psychosocial impairments associated with the condition. As noted in the DSM-III and confirmed by recent research, the average age of onset for these patients is in the mid-20s (see Figure 8), and women form the majority of clinic patients (Thyer, Parrish, Curtis, Cameron, & Nesse, 1985). The gender distribution of agoraphobia in the general population has yet to be determined. The vast majority of agoraphobics seeking treatment meet the diagnostic criteria for agoraphobia with panic attacks (DiNardo, O'Brien, Barlow, Waddell, & Blanchard, 1983; Klein, 1981; Thyer, Parrish, Curtis et al., 1985), a finding that is consistent with an important observation made by Sigmund Freud early in his career:

> In the case of agoraphobia etc., we often find the recollection of an anxiety attack; and what the patient fears is the occurrence of such an attack under the special conditions in which he believes he cannot escape it. (1962, p. 81)

Although the association between anxiety (or panic) attacks was made over 90 years ago, the significance of this association was given

Table 7:   DSM-III Criteria for Agoraphobia*

Criterion A*: The individual has marked fear of and thus avoids being alone or in public places from which escape might be difficult or help not available in case of sudden incapacitation (e.g., crowds, tunnels, bridges, public transportation).

Criterion B*: There is increasing constriction of normal activities until the fears or avoidance behavior dominate the individual's life.

Criterion C*: Not due to a major depressive episode, obsessive compulsive disorder, paranoid personality disorder, or schizophrenia.

SOURCE: American Psychiatric Association (1980, p. 227).
*Note that these criteria apply to both agoraphobia *with* panic attacks and to agoraphobia *without* panic attacks. It is the presence or absence of spontaneous panic attacks that enables the human service professional to determine which of these diagnoses is appropriate (see table 7).

little attention until an article appeared by Mendel and Klein (1969), who attributed the development and exacerbation of the *phobic* symptomatology in agoraphobia as the psychological sequelae to one or more episodes of *apparently* spontaneous panic attacks. This view was in marked contrast to the general interpretation of the agoraphobic's multiple fears in terms of symbolic displacement. Roberts (1964) describes a group of 41 agoraphobics in the following way:

> Thirty-four patients developed the initial symptoms of the illness in which they subsequently became housebound between the ages of 20 and 40. In all anxiety was the major feature in the symptoms of the illness. Without exception they all had panic attacks. Often it was the somatic and autonomic concomitants of these attacks which the patients described on admission rather than the feeling of panic, though all admitted to this when questioned. It appeared to be the fear of these recurring when the patients were out, which might result in their losing control, collapsing, fainting or making an embarrassing scene, that made them unwilling to leave their homes. Fourteen were housebound to the extent that they were unable to leave the home at all, the remainder were housebound unless they were accompanied. (p. 192)

In a preliminary study involving 28 members of an agoraphobia self-help group, each member reported having experienced one or more spontaneous panic attacks (SPA). More significantly, on the average there was a nine-year lag between the onset of the SPAs and the subsequent development of agoraphobia (Thyer & Himle, 1985). Of the sample, 79% attributed the cause of their agoraphobic fears to their apprehension over having a panic attack. Thus it would appear that Freud's original description of these patients has been well supported by contemporary research.

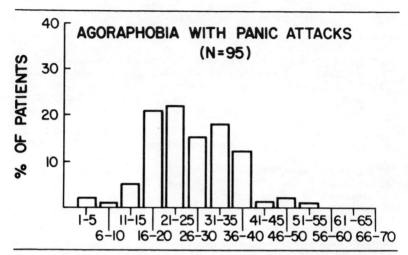

Figure 8. Distribution of the ages of onset (in five-year time periods) for 95 patients with agoraphobia with panic attacks. From Thyer, Parrish, Curtis, Nesse, and Cameron (1985, p. 117).

Another difference between the DSM-II and the DSM-III in classifying the anxiety disorders is in breaking down the earlier term "anxiety neurosis" into two distinct new categories: "panic disorder" and "generalized anxiety disorder." The individual suffering from panic disorder appears to experience SPAs identical to those associated with agoraphobia, yet does not develop phobic limitations to the same degree. The diagnosis of panic disorder is somewhat more difficult to arrive at than the disorders discussed previously, in part because the features of the condition are almost entirely subjective, internal symptoms as opposed to the outward signs associated with the phobic disorders. The diagnostic criteria for panic disorder are listed in Table 8 and obviously require very careful questioning on the part of the human service professional. It is recommended that you do not try to cover this list of symptoms from memory; rather, have a desk copy of the DSM-III at hand or develop your own checklist. A sample of such a checklist for evaluating potential panic disorder clients is presented later in this chapter. Like agoraphobia, the average age of onset for panic disorder is in the mid-20s, and the distribution of these ages of onset is also remarkably similar to that of agoraphobia (see Figure 9). The majority of panic disorder clinic patients are women, but the gender distribution of the condition in the general population is unknown.

One problem with the diagnostic criteria for panic disorder is that although apparently quantifiable estimates of symptom severity and

Table 8:   DSM-III Criteria for Panic Disorder

Criterion A: At least three panic attacks within a three-week period in circumstances other than during marked physical exertion or in a life-threatening situation. The attacks are not precipitated only by exposure to a circumscribed phobic stimulus.

Criterion B: Panic attacks are mainifested by discrete periods of apprehension or fear, and at least four of the following symptoms appear during each attack:
1. dyspnea
2. palpitations
3. chest pain or discomfort
4. choking or smothering sensations
5. dizziness, vertigo, or unsteady feelings
6. feelings of unreality
7. paresthesias (tingling in hands or feet)
8. hot and cold flashes
9. sweating
10. faintness
11. trembling or shaking
12. fear of dying, going crazy, or doing something uncontrolled during an attack

Criterion C: Not due to a physical disorder or another mental disorder, such as major depression, somatization disorder, or schizophrenia.

Criterion D: The disorder is not associated with agoraphobia.

SOURCE: American Psychiatric Association (1980, pp. 231-232).

frequency are required from the human service professional, no parameters are given to help you make these crucial decisions, forcing you to rely solely upon clinical judgment. A further vagary of the panic disorder criteria is that there are no guidelines for determining when a person no longer has panic disorder. Strictly speaking, given the present criteria a person who experienced three panic attacks within three weeks ten years ago and has not had one since would still be diagnosed as currently having panic disorder.

There are marked differences between *phobic* anxiety and the phenomenology associated with SPAs. With phobics, the client is almost always afraid of some *external* anxiety-evoking stimulus (except in the case of illness fears); away from direct and anticipated confrontation with their anxiety-evoking stimulus the phobic is generally at ease and usually indistinguishable from the nonphobic. The patient with panic disorder, however, is faced with a much different situation in that there is no external anxiety-evoking stimulus; rather, what he or she fears is an *internal* event over which he/she has no apparent control. Sheehan and his colleagues (Sheehan, 1982; Sheehan, Ballenger, & Jacobson, 1980; Sheehan & Sheehan, 1982a, 1982b) have suggested the term *endogenous anxiety* to refer to the emotions associated with apparently spontaneous panic attacks and *exogenous anxiety* for those phobic disorders associated with fears of environmental stimuli. According to a number of independent research teams (Klein, 1981; Sheehan, 1982; Thyer, Himle, Curtis et al., 1985; Turner, Williams, Mezzich, & Beidel, 1985), panic

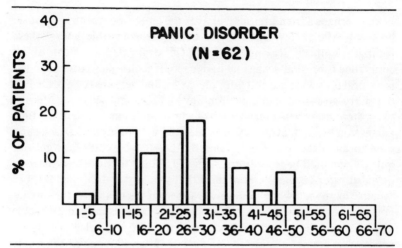

Figure 9. Distribution of the ages of onset (in five-year time periods) for 62 patients with panic disorder. From Thyer, Parrish, Curtis, Cameron, and Nesse (1985, p. 119).

disorder and agoraphobia with panic attacks are really different mani-festations of the *same condition*: the experience of spontaneous panic attacks. Why some clients experience panic attacks and subsequently develop agoraphobia whereas others continue through life with panics but develop only limited or minimal fears is an important question currently being addressed.

THE PROGRESSION OF ENDOGENOUS ANXIETY

The experience of panic attacks is a mysterious and random one. There are no known psychological or environmental precursors to their development. Imagine some time in your life when you were "frightened to death," perhaps a narrowly avoided car accident, a robbery, or a near fall. Recall the surge of panic you felt, the physical and psychological symptoms, and the gradual ebbing away of fear. With time you re-covered. Now imagine you are an incipient panic disorder patient, going about your business, driving, shopping, or perhaps relaxing at home, when suddenly, "out of the blue" you are struck with a terrifying sensation of panic and sudden, pronounced somatic symptoms (see Table 8). What is especially frightening is your lack of ability to attribute these feelings to anything. Are you having a stroke? Is this a heart attack or "the big one"? Or maybe you are going crazy! Naturally you are inclined to stop what you are doing and leave the situation and seek help—perhaps a friend, spouse, or even the emergency room at the local hospital. After a few minutes (or even a few horrible hours) these feelings diminish, leaving you shaken, drained, and most of all concerned over what it was that happened. If such attacks occur again it is natural for you to consult your physician and perhaps to be placed on the merry-go-round of doctor shopping, of being shuffled from internist to cardiologist to neurologist, each of whom pronounces you fit. As time passes you begin to avoid places associated with past panic attacks and then to anyplace where if a panic did occur, you could not get out quickly or would be terribly embarrassed. Going to the dentist, barber, or hairdresser becomes an ordeal. What would you do if one of those "spells" happened while you were trapped in the chair? At the movies you choose a seat near the exit. You may now be afraid to tackle expressway driving and limit yourself to lightly traveled secondary roads. You are not afraid of traffic per se (after all, you've been a safe driver for years) but of having a panic at high speed or far from an exit. Long tunnels, bridges, and confined spaces such as elevators or escalators are now off limits, and you shop in fast food stores so as to avoid the possibility of being caught by a panic with a loaded cart in a long checkout line. Anything that excites you, even fun things, are avoided, activities such as exercise, public speaking, sex, or arguments.

The feelings these activities engender are frighteningly similar to the initial stages of a panic attack, and you don't want to inadvertently trigger one. You may engage in ritualistic or foolish behavior because you believe it helps prevent or get rid of panic (Thyer, 1986). Early in this scenario you might have been mistakenly diagnosed as a simple or social phobic; somewhat later, as a hysteric, a case of somatization disorder, or as a hypochondriac. At another stage the diagnosis of panic disorder may have been appropriate, and now, when fears and avoidance behavior have come to dominate your life, the most correct diagnosis would be agoraphobia with panic attacks. It can be seen how the notion of a heuristic label such as Sheehan's (1982) endogenous anxiety more accurately captures this constellation of confusing signs and symptoms. In any event, however, we are left with the perplexing question: What causes panic attacks?

WHAT CAUSES APPARENTLY SPONTANEOUS PANIC ATTACKS?

For many years the prevailing perspective as to the causes of panic attacks were psychodynamic in orientation. One early theory was that panic attacks occurred in individuals who were sexually abstinent and that the episode represented a massive uncontrolled libidinal discharge (Freud, 1962). The superficial similarity between the symptoms associated with a panic attack and the symptoms of an orgasm seemed to support this notion. Of course, if this hypothesis were valid, then one would expect Catholic priests and nuns who have taken vows of celibacy to have a high proportion of panic disorder. This is not the case, and in any event this idea has not received any scientific support and has been largely discarded—perhaps unfortunately so, because the sexual abstinence theory of panic attacks suggests several interesting approaches to therapy. Additional ideas were that panic attacks leading to agoraphobia served as a defense mechanism for individuals who had unconscious desires to be sexually promiscuous. The panic attacks in this case "kept them off the streets." Libidinal impulses reared their ugly heads once more, in the theory that panic attacks leading to dependency on others and to fears of being alone served as a defense mechanism designed to protect the individual from succumbing to unconscious urges to masturbate. Again, such theories have shown a marked inability to be supported by empirical research, although on several occasions I have treated clients who had been given such interpretations of the meaning of their spontaneous panic attacks, much to their dismay, by other human service professionals they had consulted earlier.

A hypothesis that still receives some credence, and is listed in the DSM-III as a precursor to agoraphobia with panic attacks as well as for panic disorder, is the notion that "Separation Anxiety Disorder in childhood and sudden object loss apparently predispose to the development of this disorder" (American Psychiatric Association, 1980, pp. 226, 231). The evidence in support of the separation anxiety hypothesis (SAH) is generally methodologically weak and involves small samples of patients, although the symptomatic similarities between separation phenomena and panic/agoraphobia is intuitively appealing. My colleagues and I at the Anxiety Disorders Program recently conducted two studies examining the retrospectively reported incidence of childhood separation trauma in agoraphobics with panic attacks (n = 44) versus simple phobics (n = 88; see Thyer, Nesse, Curtis, & Cameron, 1985) and in patients with panic disorder (n = 23) versus simple phobics (n = 28; see Thyer, Nesse, Cameron, & Curtis, 1986). We used simple phobics as our control groups because they were clinically anxious, yet the SAH would *not* predict them to have a high incidence of childhood separation trauma. In both studies we found few or trivial differences between the two experimental groups (agoraphobic versus simple or panic disorder versus simple), and in each study our patients reported a meager history of such separation trauma. We reviewed all the available evidence pro and con the SAH; the interested reader can pursue the matter further by consulting the published articles. Although it may be true that childhood separation anxiety is a precursor to isolated cases of adult-onset panic disorder or agoraphobia, the evidence certainly does *not* support this hypothesis for the majority of patients. See also the relevant studies by Parker (1979) and Tennant, Hurray, and Bebbington (1982).

There has been much speculation in the past that patients suffering from panic attacks were actually victims of an underlying or "masked" depression, with the depressive symptomatology manifesting in the form of panics (Bowen & Kahout, 1979; Gardos, 1981 Pollitt & Young, 1971). This theory also seems unlikely to be valid. Two separate studies (Curtis, Cameron, & Nesse, 1982; Lieberman et al., 1983) administered the dexamethasone suppression test (DST) to patients with either panic disorder or agoraphobias with panic attacks or those with major depression. The DST is a sensitive blood test for detecting the abnormal neuroendocrine functioning associated with endogenous depression. In both studies the DST results indicated that panic attacks and severe depression are distinguishable disorders. It is known, however, that depression, agoraphobia, and panic disorder have a high concordance rate—in other words, panic/agoraphobia and depression often run together. Several family studies (Breir, Charney, & Heninger, 1984; Leckman, Merikangas, Gammon, & Prusoff, 1983; Leckman, Weissman, Merikangas, Pauls, & Prusoff, 1984) suggest the possibility of a common underlying pathogenic process, whereas other family studies (Crowe, Noyes, Pauls, & Slymen, 1983; Harris, Noyes, Pauls, et al., 1983) found that depression did *not* aggregate in the families of patients with panic as opposed to control subjects. It seems more likely that panic/agoraphobic clients develop depression *secondary* to the massive functional limitations they experience, as opposed to the theory that panic attacks stem from a primary depressive illness. Certainly it would be an error to assume automatically that panic disorder/agoraphobic symptomatology is the result of depression.

Although an empirical unifying theory or mechanism for panic attacks has yet to emerge, during the last few decades an intriguing body of research has produced findings that strongly suggest that spontaneous panic attacks have a *biological* etiology. This evidence has accrued along four major lines.

(1) Beginning in 1962 (Klein and Fink, 1962), it was noted that severely agoraphobic patients who had also experienced panic attacks enjoyed a marked decrease in the frequency of those attacks when treated with the then new medication imipramine (Tofranil), a tricyclic

compound usually used in the treatment of depression. This observation has been subsequently replicated (Klein, 1964; Leibowitz, 1985), and it has since been found that certain other compounds also possess antipanic properties—notably the monamine oxidase inhibitors and the newly developed triazolobenzodiazepine alprazolam (Sheehan, 1985). Briefly stated (to be elaborated on in Chapter 5), patients given an adequate trial of these compounds usually experience a significant reduction and, with careful drug management, complete relief from panic attacks. Significantly, if a patient is maintained on one of these compounds for months and then is gradually weaned from their use, panic attacks usually return.

(2) It has been shown that intravenous infusions of sodium lactate can provoke panic attacks identical to spontaneous panic attacks in patients suffering from panic disorder or agoraphobia with panic attacks. Placebo infusions have no such effect, and normal subjects are unaffected by such lactate infusions (Rainey & Nesse, 1985; Sheehan, Carr, Fishman, Walsh, & Peltier-Saxe, 1985). The substance isoproterenol possesses similar properties (Rainey, Ettedgui, Pohl, & Bridges, 1984). These lactate and isoproterenol models of panic attacks are useful tools to study the biochemical indices of panic and of potential pharmacological or psychological interventions. For example, the compounds found clinically useful in treating naturally occurring panics are found to block lactate-induced panic attacks (Fyer, Leibowitz, Gorman, Davies, & Klein, 1983; Rainey et al., 1985), whereas compounds ineffective in treating "natural" panic attacks are equally ineffective in preventing lactate-provoked ones (Gorman et al., 1984). These intriguing findings also suggest some potent biological mechanism at work.

(3) A number of family studies have recently shown that relatives of probands with either panic disorder or agoraphobia with panic attacks have an unusually high incidence of these disorders themselves. Sheehan (1982) states, "Preliminary evidence suggests that there is a greater concordance in monozygotic twins than in dizygotic twins, and that the vulnerability is transmitted genetically like an autosomal dominant gene" (p. 157).

(4) Although the research is not completely consistent, it appears that clients with panic disorder (or agoraphobia) run a significant risk for also having mitral valve prolapse syndrome (MVPS), a relatively benign heart condition (Crowe, 1985). The cause of MVPS is unknown, and the nature of the relationship between panic attacks and MVPS is also not understood. Unfortunately, patients with panic disorder have an increased risk for cardiovascular disease, compared with control

subjects matched for age and sex (Coryell, Noyes, & Clancy, 1982), although this is not known to be related to MVPS. This concordance between MVPS and panic disorder is striking and further suggestive of a biological etiology for spontaneous panic attacks.

Given the four lines of converging evidence listed above, the model suggested by Sheehan (1982) that "panic disorder is associated with a biochemical abnormality in the nervous system, to which there is a genetic vulnerability" (p. 156) seems to be the most valid of those proposed to date.

ISSUES IN DIFFERENTIAL DIAGNOSIS

As noted in Tables 7 and 8, the diagnoses of agoraphobia or panic disorder should not be used when the symptomatology is caused by physical disorders or conditions, or to another mental disorder such as obsessive-compulsive disorder, major depression, somatization disorder, paranoid personality disorder, or schizophrenia. The human service professional who has used these DSM-III citeria to arrive at a tentative diagnosis of panic disorder or agoraphobia with panic attacks should be alert for the possibility of a differential diagnosis, usually involving an underlying physical condition. (Alternative diagnoses related to mental conditions are usually not difficult to screen out.) The most common examples include hyperventilation syndrome (HVS) and hypoglycemia. It is known that hyperventilation results in an increase in anxiety and gives rise to some somatic indices associated with autonomic arousal such as tachycardia and cold extremities (Thyer, Papsdorf, & Wright, 1984). Excluding HVS as an alternative diagnosis is relatively easy and can be done by asking the client to intentionally hyperventilate when present in your office. If the symptoms produced are identical in type and magnitude to those they associate with their self-reported "panic attacks," then treatment should be directed toward the HVS itself and usually involves directive training in proper breathing (Lum, 1977). Alternatively, asking the client to breathe in and out of a paper or plastic bag held over the mouth (not the head!) when acutely anxious can also be revealing. If this produces a fairly dramatic drop in acute anxiety, then again HVS is implicated and the bag rebreathing tactic may be employed as needed. In fact, despite using a hyperventilation challenge in dozens of panic/agoraphobic clients, I have yet to see this exercise provoke a panic attack.

Many patients with panic attacks have come, usually through reading the popular literature, to believe that their panics are due to hypoglycemia. The often-used glucose-tolerance test (GTT) is actually a poor test to detect hypoglycemia (Kwentus, Achilles, & Goyer, 1982; McDonald, Fisher, & Burnham, 1965) and is of little use in ruling out this differential diagnosis. The only "hard" evidence on this matter comes from a study of 10 patients with panic disorder who were given a lactate infusion to provoke a panic attack. At the point of panic all patients had their blood sugar levels tested, and *no* patient was found to be remotely near a state of hypoglycemia (Gorman, Martinez, Leibowitz, Fyer, & Klein, 1984). True, an episode of hypoglycemia (perhaps caused by fasting) may produce symptoms akin to those of panic, causing an otherwise anxious client to fear that a full-blown panic episode is beginning, but the magnitude of symptoms associated with hypoglycemia never reaches those of a panic attack. Several years ago I served as a medical volunteer in an experiment that involved my taking a large dose of insulin by injection, a dose sufficient to drop my blood sugar to 35 mg/dl, hypoglycemic by any standard. I developed a minor tremor and some jitteriness but certainly not a panic attack.

Although acute stages of caffeine or other drug intoxication may mimic a panic episode, because the precipitant is usually so easy to isolate, mistaken diagnoses of these states are rare.

A number of other physical conditions can give rise to periodic paniclike states, conditions such as vestibular dysfunction (Caplan, 1983), thyroid problems (Lindeman, Zitrin, & Klein, 1984), and organic mental disorders (Dietch, 1984). Patients with such serious conditions often screen themselves out prior to consulting the nonmedical human service professional through their often frantic efforts to find an organic cause for their panics. It goes without saying that if there is any doubt as to the validity of a panic disorder or agoraphobic diagnosis in a patient who has not received a complete medical evaluation, then such a referral should be made promptly. Human service professionals in the field of anxiety disorders would be well served by thoroughly reviewing recent works pertaining to differential diagnoses for these conditions (e.g., Cameron, 1985).

Occasionally a client appears who apparently meets the criteria for agoraphobia *without* panic attacks. At our clinic we often found that such patients were suffering from some somatic ailment of an unpredictable or spasmotic nature, such as epilepsy or colitis (Thyer, Himle, Curtis, Cameron, & Nesse, 1985). In these cases the physical illness served as the functional equivalent of spontaneous panic attacks, in terms of producing agoraphobic-like restrictions. In other words, the epileptic's seizures and anticipation of these leads to avoidance behaviors similar to those associated with agoraphobia, (e.g., public places where escape might be difficult or help unavailable in case of sudden incapacitation, or where the client might be embarrassed). A similar case can be made for the victims of colitis, perhaps even more strongly. The works of Pinto (1972), Mittan (1983), and Clouse and Lustman (1983) support these views. In such cases the underlying somatic disorder needs to be appropriately addressed.

There has been much speculation in the literature that marital relationship factors may contribute to the development and maintenance of agoraphobia without panic attacks. In general, such hypotheses have not received much empirical support (Arrindell & Emmelkamp, 1985; Vandereycken, 1983). Regardless, if the human service professional obtains evidence implicating marital or familial pathology in maintaining agoraphobic avoidance behavior, it is then clearly appropriate to refer for or to provide marital or family therapy.

ASSESSMENT AIDS

A number of self-report inventories have been developed for use with clients suffering from agoraphobia or panic disorder. Because of the more complex nature of these disorders, the assessment tools are of necessity more complex. To make a diagnosis of agoraphobia is not usually difficult (see Table 7), given the pervasiveness with which the disorder dominates the individual's life.

The question of making an accurate determination concerning the quality and quantity of suspected panic attacks, necessary to a diagnosis of panic disorder or agoraphobia, is appreciably more difficult (see Table 8). To aid the human service professional in evaluating potential panic attacks, my colleagues at the Anxiety Disorders Program at the University of Michigan Hospitals have developed a Panic Attack Questionnaire (PAQ) for clinician use as a form to be completed with each client (See Table 9). The first page of the PAQ will help you determine if the client's paniclike experiences meet the *quantitative* criteria enumerated by the DSM-III (i.e., at least three spontaneous panic attacks within any three-week period of an individual's life). The question of spontaneity can be a difficult one to evaluate, and the issue here is to determine carefully whether or not the episodes take the client by surprise. If panic can be reliably evoked by environmental stimuli (e.g., driving, public speaking, shopping), then the phenomenon the client is referring to is more properly labeled "phobic anxiety," not a panic attack. This distinction is crucial because SPAs and phobic anxiety often require completely different approaches to treatment. Note, however, that phobic anxiety can be just as intense and frightening as are SPAs, only the triggering mechanism is different.

Page two of the PAQ helps you to make a *qualitative* determination concerning the nature of a client's panic attacks. For an episode to be legitimately labeled a panic attack, the client must have experienced at least four of the 12 symptoms listed on page two of the PAQ. You are limited to the client's retrospective reports of panic episodes that may have occurred months or weeks in the past, which is a disadvantage compared to evaluating patients with concurrent affective disturbances such as severe depression or generalized anxiety disorder, because the client can more accurately report present symptomatology as opposed to past feeling states. Accordingly, you must simply do your best in covering each potential symptom, and if there is any doubt as to whether or not a client understands your terminology, rephrase the question using more colloquial language. This has been done, in part, on the PAQ, substituting "shortness of breath" for "dyspnea," "awareness of your heart beating" for "palpitations," and so on. When completed, the PAQ enables the human service professional to make an accurate determination of whether or not the client meets the quantitative and qualitative diagnostic criteria for panic disorder. The final caveat is that rarely some patients with panic attacks experience all of the physical symptoms of panics but do not make a presenting complaint of emotional upset (Jones, 1984). Such individuals possibly account for the mislabeling of some panic disorder patients as instances of somatization disorder, hysteria, or hypochondriasis (Sheehan & Sheehan, 1982a).

The measurement of agoraphobia may also be accomplished through using several standardized self-report measures. The Fear Survey Schedule described in Chapter 2 has a subscale of items that have been empirically shown to discriminate agoraphobic clients from those with other anxiety disorders (Arrindell, 1980). The Symptom Checklist (SCL-90) also has an agoraphobia subscale included in it (Derogatis, Lipman, & Covi, 1973), as does the Marks and Mathews (1979) one-page Fear Questionnaire. Any of these measures can be independently completed by clients prior to their initial interview in order to provide you with a preliminary assessment of their condition.

More recently, Chambless, Caputo, Jasin, Gracely, and Williams (1985) published an innovative instrument called the Mobility Inventory for Agoraphobia (MIA). This self-report measure asks clients to

Table 9:   The Panic Attack Questionnaire*

Page 1

Client Name: _____   Date: _____

Have you *ever* had attacks of anxiety, fear, or pain which   Yes ☐   No ☐
come suddenly, unexpectedly, or for no apparent reason?
(Continue with the remaining questions if the client responds yes to the above.)

Are these attacks mainly during physical exertion (that is,   Yes ☐   No ☐
they don't usually occur at other times)?

Please describe any other event, situation, object, etc., in which these attacks seem
likely to occur.

_____

_____

_____

Please tell me the approximate date when you first began to have these attacks
(month and year). _____

What was your age at that time? _____

Please tell me the approximate date of your last attack. _____

Do you still have these attacks?   Yes ☐   No ☐

If so, please tell me how often you have them now, i.e., how many times:
per day_____   in a week _____   in a month_____   in a year_____

About how long do they usually last now, i.e., how many:
              minutes _____   hours _____   days _____

Were they ever more frequent than they are now?   Yes ☐   No ☐

If so, how often did you have them when they were at their worst, i.e., how many
times: per day _____   in a week _____   in a month _____   in a year _____

What percentage of these attacks are "spontaneous;" that is, they seem to come
on for no apparent reason, or take you by surprise?   _____ percent

indicate the degree to which they avoid a number of potentially phobic
situations or places due to anxiety. Clients are asked to rate their
avoidance of these anxiety-evoking stimuli separately for when they are
accompanied and also for when they are alone. A brief measure of the
frequency of panic attacks is also provided. The MIA possesses
impressive reliability and validity data, and in my opinion this
instrument is the single best assessment instrument which may be used in
the evaluation of agoraphobia clients. Two related measures have also
been developed by Chambless, Caputo, Bright, and Gallagher (1984):
the Body Sensations Questionnaire and the Agoraphobic Cognitions
Questionnaire. The first provides a measure of the *bodily sensations* an
agoraphobic experiences when anxious; the second, of his or her

Table 9   Continued

During these attacks do you usually experience or feel:

Yes	No		
____	____	1.	Short of breath?
____	____	2.	Awareness of your heart beating?
____	____	3.	Pain or discomfort in your chest?
____	____	4.	Choking or smothering feelings?
____	____	5.	Dizziness, spinning sensations, or unsteady feelings?
____	____	6.	Things around you seem unreal or like a dream?
____	____	7.	You or your body seem unreal, detached, or not present?
____	____	8.	Numbness or tingling in hands or feet?
____	____	9.	Hot or cold flashes?
____	____	10.	Sweating?
____	____	11.	Faintness?
____	____	12.	Trembling or shaking?
____	____	13.	Fear of dying, of going crazy, or of doing something out of control?

*The Panic Attack Questionnaire was developed by George C. Curtis, M.D., Anxiety Disorders Program, Department of Psychiatry, University of Michigan Hospitals, Ann Arbor, MI 48109, and is reproduced by permission.

thoughts concerning the negative consequences of experiencing anxiety. Both of these instruments are also easy for the client to complete and for the clinician to evaluate and may be useful for clinical applications.

A final assessment tool worth mentioning is the Anxiety Disorders Interview Schedule (ADIS) published by DiNardo and associates (1983). The ADIS is a structured interview that a clinician follows to guide his or her evaluation of a client with a potential anxiety disorder. Detailed responses are obtained concerning a client's situational and cognitive cues that give rise to anxiety, intensity of anxiety, extent of avoidance, precipitating events, and history of the problem. All of the DSM-III criteria for adult anxiety disorders are covered by the ADIS, and this format is the best effort to date in providing assistance to the human service professional in diagnosing the anxious client. A drawback to the ADIS is that the entire interview protocol requires approximately 90 minutes to complete, which may be impractical for some human service settings. The obvious clinical value of the ADIS, coupled with its good psychometric properties, causes me to recommend it strongly.

Chapter 5

AGORAPHOBIA AND PANIC DISORDER
Treatment Strategies

The experience of overcoming fear is extraordinarily delightful.

—Bertrand Russell

Prior to beginning any discussion on effective treatments for agoraphobia, it is important that the human service professional make a clear distinction between three separate but interconnected manifestations of anxiety in agoraphobic and panic disorder clients. The first concept is that of the anxiety that occurs during a *panic attack*. This is the transient yet incredibly terrifying experience described in the previous chapter. In one of his early cases, cited in *Studies in Hysteria*, Freud related the following description of a panic attack, described for him by an 18-year-old woman: "It suddenly comes upon me. There is first a pressure upon my eyes. My head becomes so heavy that it hums so that I can hardly bear it, and then my chest begins to press together so that I cannot get my breath . . . the throat becomes laced together as if choked . . . I always feel 'Now, I must die,' . . . on the day that I have this attack, I do not trust myself anywhere" (Breuer & Freud, 1895/1966). By reviewing the criteria for panic attacks listed in Table 8, we see that this woman's experience contains the following five symptoms: dyspnea (shortness of breath), chest pain or discomfort, choking or smothering sensations, and the fear of dying. Because only four of the 12 symptoms listed in Criterion B are required to label the experience as a panic attack, we are justified in assuming that her episode may be accurately described as such. Other clients with panic attacks may experience a completely different list of symptoms; thus the human service professional needs to be familiar with all of the diagnostic criteria. The features that seem most typical of panic attacks are their sudden, unexpected onset and the sensation that one is dying. Recall that panic attacks occur randomly and are *not* a reaction to environmental events. By definition all panic disorder and most agoraphobic patients experience such episodes. If they occur frequently enough, the individual may develop marked *anticipatory anxiety*, dreading the next such episode of panic.

Days or weeks may pass without a panic attack, yet symptomatically the client may still appear in a high state of apprehension. Often he or she is unable to articulate what is causing the anxiousness, vaguely referring to something bad happening or that he or she might die. This is understandable given the terrifying nature of panics.

If the experience of panic attacks has led to the development of circumscribed or limited fears, the correct diagnosis is still panic disorder, although some clinicians refer to these presentations as mixed phobias. The most frequent of these limited fears are to highway driving, of enclosed spaces, or of public speaking. It is crucial that clients complaining of circumscribed phobias be carefully screened for a history of panic attacks, in order that the human service professional not mistakenly diagnose such individuals as suffering from simple or social phobia. When such *phobic avoidance* comes to dominate the client's life, the correct diagnosis becomes agoraphobia with panic attacks. The agoraphobic with panic attacks thus presents with all three aspects of anxiety: panic attacks, anticipatory anxiety, and phobic avoidance; the agoraphobic without panic attacks presents with only two aspects; anticipatory anxiety and phobic avoidance. Clients with panic disorder present with panic attacks and anticipatory anxiety, although a limited amount of phobic avoidance may be present. Zitrin, Woerner, and Klein (1981) and Klein (1981) discuss these distinctions in further detail. It has been proposed that the DSM-IV revise this system in favor of one delineating panic disorder (uncomplicated), panic disorder with agoraphobia, and panic disorder with limited phobic avoidance (Spitzer & Williams, 1985). Given that agoraphobia with panic attacks represents the most complex of the currently established disorders, treatment strategies for this condition will be discussed first.

TREATMENT STRATEGIES

There is an unresolved debate in the mental health field over the best effective treatment for clients who are agoraphobic and have concurrent panic attacks. The controversy concerns the relative effectiveness of medications and psychosocial interventions such as therapeutic exposure. Evidence of this debate can be obtained by reading the February 1983 issue of the *Archives of General Psychiatry*, one of the most prestigious psychiatric journals. Two major outcome studies were published side by side, reporting the results of well-controlled experiments involving imipramine hydrochloride versus behavior therapy, versus the two approaches combined, in the treatment of severe agoraphobics. Marks and associates (1983) found that real-life therapeutic exposure worked extremely well at reducing the frequency of panic attacks and removing phobic limitations, whereas imipramine alone was ineffective and imipramine plus exposure was no more effective that exposure alone. In contrast, Zitrin et al. (1983) found imipramine to be very effective at reducing the frequency of panic attacks. Following relief from panics, patients could be readily encouraged to reenter phobic situations and lose their fearful limitations. The next few issues of the *Archives of General Psychiatry* contained vigorous discussions by the authors of these works, as well as by other parties, to account for these discrepant results, but the issue is not resolved and will be discussed in the section below on pharmacotherapy. In all fairness it should be noted that both pharmacological and psychosocial treatments have received substantial support as effective therapies for agoraphobia.

PSYCHOSOCIAL TREATMENT FOR AGORAPHOBIA

In 1918, Freud made the following observation:

> The various forms of disease treated by us cannot all be addressed by the same technique.... The phobias have already made it necessary for us to go beyond our former limits.... One must proceed differently. Take the case of agoraphobia; there are two classes of it, one mild and the other severe. Patients belonging to the first class suffer from anxiety when they go into the street by themselves, but they have not yet given up going out alone on that account; the others protect themselves from the anxiety by altogether ceasing to go about alone. With these last one succeeds only when one can induce them by the influence of the analysis to behave like phobic patients of the first class—that is to go into the street and to struggle with the anxiety while they make the attempt. (1918/1962, pp. 165-166).

This approach, based upon prolonged exposure to anxiety-evoking situations, was largely ignored in favor of purely verbal therapies until the past two decades. In recent years psychosocial treatments based on therapeutic exposure have received an impressive degree of empirical support. Jansson and Ost (1982) recently conducted a review of this literature and found 24 published controlled experimental studies, involving a total of 652 agoraphobic patients, with follow-up periods of up to nine years. Real-life exposure was a key ingredient in 71% of these studies, causing Jansson and Ost to conclude, "approximately 60-70%

of the patients treated with exposure in vivo showed clinically significant improvements in agoraphobic problems immediately after treatment, and at six-month follow-up. Further, there was better experimental support for the more direct exposure treatments as compared to the indirect exposure methods" (1982, p. 311). Recalling that only a few years ago agoraphobia was notoriously intractible to *any* form of treatment, these results are indeed most encouraging.

Initially behavioral treatments for agoraphobia consisted of systematic desensitization in imagination, which yielded modest results (Cooper, 1963; Marks & Gelder, 1965; Wolpe, 1958). Early reports on the success of therapeutic exposure conducted in real-life contexts as a treatment for agoraphobia (Meyer, 1957) stimulated comparative studies contrasting exposure in imagination versus exposure in real life. The evidence was clear: Real-life practice was statistically and clinically superior to systematic desensitization in fantasy (Crowe et al., 1972; Emmelkamp & Wessels, 1975; Johnston et al., 1976). As in the treatment of simple and social phobias, it has been shown that *intensive* real-life practice (ten daily sessions of two hours each) produces results superior to 10 such practice sessions spaced a week apart (Foa, Jameson, Turner, & Payne, 1980). These studies evaluating the effects of individually conducted, therapist-assisted exposure therapy were followed by research on the effectiveness of real-life exposure with a therapist but conducted in small group contexts (the possible advantage of group treatment being that a given human service professional could provide care for a greater number of clients). Such groups have been found to yield positive results comparable to individually conducted treatment sessions. An additional benefit is that the use of a group context fosters feelings of cohesion and support among the group members, which apparently facilitates the exposure process (Hand, Lamontagne, & Marks, 1974; Teasdale, Walsh, Lancashire, & Mathews, 1977; Watson, Mullett, & Pillay, 1973). Community-based self-help groups, established with a focus on encouraging an individual's self-conducted and group exposure practice, are also being found to benefit agoraphobic clients (Jannoun, Munby, Catalan, & Gelder, 1980; Mathews, Johnston, Shaw, & Gelder, 1974; Thyer, 1985a; Sinnott, Jones, Scott-Fordham, & Woodward, 1981). Community-based self-help groups of this nature convey the joint advantages of extending the therapeutic resources of the human service professional and bring treatment opportunities closer to the client, an especially important consideration in work with agoraphobics. An additional benefit is the effect of modeling of courageous behavior by recovering group members on the self-help efforts of the less recovered or more impaired group member.

The overall treatment strategy for agoraphobics is similar to that outlined in Chapter 3 for the care of simple and social phobics. The first step is careful client education about the nature of panic attacks and how the development of agoraphobia is a natural consequence of such experiences. It is useful to have a stock of handouts and readings for client use in this regard. Similarly a supply of self-help books (e.g., Marks, 1978; Mathews, Gelders, & Johnston, 1981; Weekes, 1979; Zane & Milt, 1984) should be available for clients to purchase or borrow. I have found local bookstores to be most cooperative in this respect by keeping such books in stock, particularly after I sent a steady stream of clients their way. Such materials, as with simple and social phobics, provide accurate information to clients about the nature of their disorder, describe encouraging case histories of recovered agoraphobics, and outline general treatment strategies. This initial stage of treatment is also devoted towards developing a working therapeutic alliance with the client.

Stimulus mapping, determining the critical features of the multiple situations that a given agoraphobic client fears, is somewhat more complex than with simple and social phobics. As described in Chapter 3, with the assistance of the client, prepare a list of these feared circumstances and ask the client to rank them in order of their anxiety-evoking potential. The Mobility Inventory for agoraphobics described in Chapter 4 can be helpful in this regard, as is careful interviewing technique. The human service professional should never arbitrarily plan to initiate exposure therapy with a new client based upon some preconceived notion regarding what it is that agoraphobics are afraid of, since there is great diversity in terms of the parameters of agoraphobic fears.

Another technique used in stimulus mapping is to have the client keep ongoing daily diaries or logs enumerating two distinct factors: the frequency of panic attacks, and real-life exposure activities. Tables 10 and 11 depict sample blank pages from such diaries, and you can provide the client with a small supply of these prior to beginning treatment. It is important for you to educate the client regarding the distinction to be made between a spontaneous panic attack and situationally induced anxiety caused by actually being in frightening circumstances, or anticipating an imminent venture out of one's "safe zone." Shortly after each paniclike episode, have the client indicate on the form the symptoms he or she may have experienced and describe the nature of the episode (unexpected versus anticipated panic), its duration (in minutes), and the intensity of the attack (1 = mild, 10 = worst ever). Stress the importance of this information for the proper understanding and

Table 10:   Panic Attack Diary

Panic Attack Diary				
Name: _____			Date: _____	
Time of Panic	Expected (E) or Unexpected OU	Duration (in minutes)	Intensity (1-10)	Symptoms Experienced*

*Symptom List (put the correct numbers for the symptoms you experienced under the symptom column for each separate panic attack).
1.   shortness of breath
2.   palpitations
3.   chest pain or discomfort
4.   choking or smothering sensations
5.   dizziness, vertigo, or unsteady feelings
6.   feelings of unreality
7.   tingling in hands or feet
8.   hot or cold flashes
9.   sweating
10.   faintness
11.   trembling or shaking
12.   fear of dying, going crazy, or doing something out of control

treatment of the client. In truth, without such detailed information the human service professional often finds it difficult to evaluate the efficacy of a treatment program or to detect subtle changes in the client's condition, given the complex nature of agoraphobia and the myriad complaints and worries agoraphobics often express.

Clients may state that their fears wax and wane for no apparent reason; certain activities are relatively easy on some days and exceedingly difficult on others. Such phobic exacerbations are often related to ongoing life events (family discord, illness, etc.). Caffeine use may need to be monitored or reduced given evidence that clients with panic attacks are often acutely sensitive to the anxiety-evoking properties of

Table 11:   Homework Diary

Homework Diary

Name: _____   Date: _____

I did the following homework activity:

I was ___ alone; ___ with someone (Who? _____).
I practiced for ___ minutes.
My highest level of anxiety during my practice was ___ (0 = calm, 100 = panic)
Additional comments:

_____

I did the following homework activity:

I was ___ alone; ___ with someone (Who? _____).
I practiced for ___ minutes.
My highest level of anxiety during my practice was ___.
Additional comments:

_____

this substance (Charney et al., 1985). Other times you may need to accompany the client into the actual real-life situations they fear in order to isolate accurately the anxiety-provoking factors. A walk together through a bank or supermarket may be found by the agoraphobic client to be quite easy, but if you have them transact banking business with a teller or purchase a cart full of groceries, the experience is terrifying. The reason is the subtle distinction between a situation from which the client can escape easily in case of panic and one in which the client is "trapped." You can always walk out of a bank or store without embarrassment, *unless* you are waiting for the teller to count out some change or for the clerk to total your purchases. It is distinctions of this caliber that the human service professional needs to be aware of as operative in eliciting anxiety in the client and to structure exposure practice properly. One client of mine enumerated his list of fears: public speaking, shopping, expressway driving, and crowded theaters. I asked him if there were any other fears, which he denied. I then said, "How do you feel about barber shops?" My client's eyes widened and he stared at me for several moments, finally stammering out, "How did you know that? I have never told anyone but I am frightened to death of having my hair cut by a barber. My wife has cut mine for the past three years."

Because I had realized that all of his fears involved situations from which escape would be difficult (in the event of a panic attack), I simply chose another common experience incorporating a similar factor, thus giving the impression of omniscience. This process of stimulus mapping is ongoing throughout the course of treatment, revised as the client learns to perceive more accurately his or her anxiety-evoking stimuli and reveals more information to the human service professional.

My preference is that the first few attempts at therapeutic exposure with an agoraphobic be conducted with the accompaniment and guidance of the human service professional. As before, ask the client to pick a moderately challenging exposure task from the list of anxiety-evoking situations derived from the stimulis-mapping procedure. Teach the client how to report his or her feelings of anxiety using a 0 (completely calm) to 100 (panic-stricken) point scale and accompany him or her as the chosen task is attempted. As an example, let us say that a client is frightened of walking away from home. Walk with her down the sidewalk, using the regular aids of support, reassurance, and encouragement, and periodically ask her to rate her level of fear. When the client begins to balk, saying that she cannot go any further or that she wishes to retrace her route home, persuade her to remain where she is, talking with you. Distracting conversation, cajoling, and humor are all tools that may be appropriately employed for this task. With the passage of a few minutes, almost inevitably the client will begin to calm down and report decreasing levels of anxiety. Verbally reinforce her for having the courage to remain with you. If possible, choose a convenient place to rest, such as a park bench or a plaza where you can sit. When the client is adequately calmed, you need to judge if you should suggest continuing further on in that session or returning home. The valuable lesson clients learn from these sessions is that with sufficiently long exposure, their anxiety will *decrease*, not escalate into panic. Because agoraphobics almost always flee the scene when they get frightened, it comes as quite a surprise for them to learn that the sensations of anticipatory anxiety do not indicate the imminent outbreak of a panic attack.

A given route or task should be repeatedly accomplished until the client finds it relatively easy to complete, if not actually boring. At that point you should begin shaping greater independence in the client. Using the example of walking away from home, once the client can easily do this with your accompaniment, suggest and obtain permission to *follow* her from some set distance behind; practice this until the distance is considerable yet the client is comfortable. Then suggest that you remain in one spot while she goes out by herself, gradually increasing her radius. Following the successful accomplishment of this task, arrange to meet the client someplace, and so on. At this point the client has had a number of successful, confidence-building trials of accomplishing some formerly frightening task; now is the time to begin practicing the task in your absence, as a homework assignment practiced *in between* treatment sessions with you. The homework practice form in Table 11 should be used to keep track of these client efforts.

At the beginning of each new treatment session review the client's homework reports since the last time you met. The judicious use of praise and reinforcement should follow reports of successful practice exercises, and those the client failed to undertake despite his or her commitment to do so or that resulted in a premature retreat due to anxiety should be reviewed to see if the task is too big a step from the last one successfully accomplished.

Obviously, therapeutic exposure is a psychosocial intervention that cannot be conducted exclusively from the confines of the human service professional's office. You must go out into the real-world context where your client lives, make frequent home visits, and in general abandon the traditions of consulting room practice. Mutual bus rides, visits to shopping malls and grocery stores, and highway driving sessions are common during the initial stages of treatment. Occasionally you will be taxed to come up with an appropriate task for the client to undertake, some activity that is neither too big a step forward, nor altogether too easy. With the passage of time and client successes, you can begin to fade yourself out of the picture, however, encouraging the client to practice more and more autonomously.

Occasionally it is possible to treat several agoraphobics with similar limitations in joint sessions. With client permission you can arrange small group meetings. The therapeutic potential of introducing two or more agoraphobics, each of whom thought he or she was the only one afflicted with these bizarre fears, cannot be overestimated. In some social service settings it is possible to initiate an agoraphobia self-help group (Thyer, 1985a), whose members may either meet at a local agency's conference room or less formally, perhaps rotating among the group members' homes. For one and a half years I facilitated such an agoraphobia self-help group, and the weekly group meetings held in a hospital conference room usually had about 20 individuals in attendance. Once introduced, members can be encouraged to engage in homework practice together or arrange joint field trips. Another such self-help group I am familiar with meets in a Detroit suburb and averages over 100 persons in attendance each week. A regular program is followed, with a new speaker (usually a human service professional knowledgeable in the field of anxiety) each week. Field trips are arranged and conducted by recovered agoraphobics, and a telephone "panic hotline" exists in which group members can turn to trained volunteers for reassurance.

SPECIAL PROBLEMS

Client compliance with agreed-upon homework tasks represents the most potentially troublesome aspect of the conduct of therapeutic exposure. The human service professional must be most insistent upon this point, because without such practice little progress can be made. In general you can guard against problems of client noncompliance by a careful use of the therapeutic alliance, by initially working closely with the client and then slowly fading yourself out of the picture during exposure sessions. By carefully attending to clients' reports of their homework and by going over the homework practice forms (see Table 11), you reinforce the importance of this aspect of their rehabilitation. It is especially important not to push clients faster than they are willing to proceed. In extreme cases of noncompliance, oral or written contingency contracts may be resorted to (Shelton & Levy, 1981). Compliance with therapeutic tasks as a condition of treatment is by no means an unusual requirement in psychotherapy (Herzberg, 1941; Omer, 1985), and the human service professional working with agoraphobic clients need not be reluctant to facilitate such adherence. Fortunately, the client dropout rate with exposure therapy is comparable to that obtained with conventional verbal psychotherapy (Marks, 1981).

Occasionally agoraphobic clients will have a set of established partial avoidance behaviors designed to reduce the aversiveness of phobic confrontations. Such activities tend to hinder complete desensitization and, although permissible during the early stages of treatment, should be given up as soon as possible. Obvious examples of such avoidance activities are alcohol or drug abuse, problems that ideally should be addressed prior to attempts to treat agoraphobia. Clients should be encouraged to give up carrying small quantities of alcohol or tranquilizers, taken along "just in case," and to desist from other activities designed to reduce anxiety. Such anxiety-reducing rituals often take on aspects of superstitious conditioning (Thyer, 1986); clients may carry containers of ice or damp rags to wipe their brow if anxious. Sunglasses, canes, umbrellas or large purses also are often used to give the client comfort. Eventually these must be discarded.

Although exposure therapy is established to be the treatment of choice in helping clients overcome the limitations of phobic avoidance, it is less clear how this treatment effects the course of spontaneous panic attacks. Marks and associates (Cohen, Monteiro, & Marks, 1984; Marks et al., 1983) claim that exposure alone is an effective treatment for agoraphobia with panic attacks and that as clients progress "the number and intensity of panic attacks are reduced as well as the avoidance" (Marks, 1983a, p. 1151). It is not uncommon, however, for a client to make good progress in decreasing phobic avoidance through exposure treatments and then to regress somewhat following another spontaneous panic attack, necessitating additional work to regain lost ground. Setbacks may occur, but with proper prior client education and therapist support these need not be viewed as a sign of treatment failure but as an anticipated component of the rehabilitation process.

PHARMACOLOGICAL TREATMENTS FOR AGORAPHOBIA

Another avenue of approach for treating agoraphobia with panic attacks is pharmacological in nature, requiring the nonmedical human service professional to refer and collaborate with a psychiatrist knowledgeable in contemporary psychopharmacology. There is now good evidence that panic attacks (but not anticipatory anxiety or phobic avoidance) can be temporarily alleviated with treatment with either one of the tricyclic antidepressant medications, most commonly imipramine (Leibowitz, 1985), one of the monoamine-oxidase inhibitors, most commonly phenelzine (Sheehan, 1985), and a newer one of the benzodiazepine compounds, alprazolam (Sheehan, 1985). The most common theory among biological psychiatrists is that because agoraphobia is secondary to panic attacks, clients need pharmacological treatment to relieve these panics, at which point they can then successfully be coaxed into undertaking therapeutic exposure activities. In a major review of this literature Marks (1983a) provides evidence that these so-called antipanic medications may be effective only with patients who suffer from a concurrent affective illness, such as severe depression. Recent outcome studies have shown that combining pharmacological treatment with exposure therapy is no more effective than rigorous exposure therapy by itself (Marks et al., 1983; Mavissakalian & Michelson, 1983; Michelson & Mavissakalian, 1985; Telch, Agras, Taylor, Roth, & Ballen, 1985).

Treatment of agoraphobia with medication appears to have some drawbacks. Some clients (10%-25%) simply cannot tolerate the side effects of some of these antipanic compounds, and in the absence of careful physician management this may lead to higher dropout rates than with the psychosocial therapies. Second, pharmacological treatments are purely ameliorative. Just like a diabetic who takes insulin to control the ravages of diabetes, the agoraphobic on medication is protected from panics, but if medication is discontinued relapse rates are high, in contrast to the well-maintained gains obtained with exposure therapy. On balance it seems most appropriate initially to attempt to treat agoraphobics with therapeutic exposure alone, and only if significant benefits are not forthcoming should the human service professional contemplate the adjunctive use of medication.

TREATING AGORAPHOBIA WITHOUT PANIC ATTACKS

For those few clients who meet the criteria for agoraphobia without panic attacks, we have found that this group "often suffered from some somatic ailment of an unpredictable or spasmotic nature, such as epilepsy or colitis. This physical illness often served as the functional equivalent to panic attacks in terms of developing agoraphobic restrictions"(Thyer, Himle, Curtis, Cameron, & Nesse, 1985, p. 209). As an example of this process, it is known that epileptics often develop agoraphobic-like avoidance behavior and anticipatory anxiety due to experiences or fears of having a seizure in a public setting (Mittan, 1983; Pinto, 1972). It would not require many episodes of having an attack of spastic colitis in public and resultant soiling of oneself with feces for such an individual to "avoid public places from which escape might be difficult," and thus symptomatically meet the criteria for agoraphobia. Clark (1963) describes a client who developed agoraphobia without panic attacks secondary to an embarrassing facial spasm. Such clients should first be effectively treated for the underlying somatic ailment (e.g., antiseizure medication in the case of an epileptic), at which point the standard practices of exposure therapy may be initiated.

PSYCHOSOCIAL TREATMENTS FOR PANIC DISORDER

As described above, there is good evidence that therapeutic exposure alone can reduce the frequency and intensity of spontaneous panic attacks. This finding has no logical bearing on the likelihood that these panics have a biological origin, as reviewed in Chapter 4. Some biological disorders are known to respond well to psychosocial therapies, whereas certain psychological conditions are best treated with biological interventions. The antipanic effects of exposure seem secondary to the beneficial influence such treatments have on phobic anxiety and anticipatory anxiety, given that, as will be recalled, spontaneous panic attacks have no identifiable anxiety-evoking stimulus that can be re-created for the purposes of exposure work. Guttmacher and Nelles (1984) gave a lactate challenge test to a panic patient, who indeed panicked. This individual was subsequently treated with therapeutic exposure and a placebo medication. At the end of six weeks of this regimen, the patient underwent a lactate challenge test identical to the first, only this time the procedure did not produce a panic attack in the patient. Given that tolerance to the panicogenic effects of sodium lactate had previously been reported only through the use of medication (Rifkin, 1983), this finding that a client treated only with exposure also demonstrates that resistance to lactate challenge testing is a most important result that, we hope, will be replicated.

In an interview and observational study, Ley (1985) found that hyperventilation symptoms appeared prior to the onset of fears in nine out of ten patients with panic attacks. Observation of six of these ten subjects' breathing suggested that all six had resting respiration rates significantly higher than the rate for the normal population. Given that hyperventilation can produce paniclike effects (Thyer, Papsdorf, & Wright, 1984), various respiratory or breathing retraining procedures have been employed with clients suffering from panic disorder. Cooke (1979) describes a case history wherein panics were completely alleviated through the use of breathing exercises and client education. Rapee (1985) describes a similar case history, documented with data, that breathing retraining reduced the frequency and intensity of his client's panic attacks. Clark, Salkovskis, and Chalkley (1985) treated 18 clients with panic attacks using respiratory control techniques and employed an interrupted time-series research design. Following three weeks of baseline monitoring of panic frequency, respiratory control training was instituted for two weeks. Panic attacks were monitored for the next 11 weeks and at 6- and 24-month follow-up. It was shown that the respiratory control procedure resulted in significant reductions in panic frequency and phobic avoidance. This study is of particular importance because it is one of the few controlled group experiments demonstrating the effectiveness of a psychological intervention on panic attacks.

Using a multiple baseline design across three subjects, Waddell, Barlow, & O'Brien (1984) reported that cognitive therapy combined with relaxation training effectively reduced panic attacks. The cognitive therapy consisted of self-statement training designed to help clients engage in anxiety-alleviating as opposed to anxiety-increasing cognitions. Another cognitive strategy was to teach clients how to keep their attention focused on a particular task, as opposed to somatic symptoms of anxiousness. Barlow et al. (1984) treated 11 panic disorder patients with relaxation training combined with electromyographic biofeedback and cognitive therapy. At posttreatment two of the 11 patients reported essentially no panic attacks, and the remainder reported that their panics were less frequent, less severe, and shorter. These improvements were maintained at a one-year follow-up. The experimental design did not permit the researchers to determine which of the components of the treatment program was responsible for these improvements, however.

It should be noted that some clients undergoing relaxation training experience a paradoxical transient *increase* in anxiety (Heide & Borkovec, 1984). Thus it is important that the human service professional electing to employ this procedure be alert to this possibility. Unfortunately, there are no studies that demonstrate that relaxation training alone has any influence on panic disorder patients.

Several researchers have attempted to desensitize panic clients to the experience of panic attacks through the artificial induction of paniclike states. Orwin (1973) attempted this by having his patient vigorously exercise during exposure therapy, giving rise to hyperventilation, tachycardia, tremor, perspiration, and shortness of breath. This case history reported good results. Griez and van den Hout (1983) tried to desensitize their patient to panic attacks by having him inhale a 35% carbon dioxide/65% oxygen mixture, which was found to provoke panics. This was repeated 10 times per day for five days and followed by three weeks of exposure therapy. Interestingly enough, after the second day of inhalation-induced panics, the client became completely desensitized to them and reported that he was no longed frightened during the experience. Part of the exposure treatment subsequently consisted of having him spend a week in a foreign country whose language he did not speak. Six-month follow-up revealed continued reductions in panic frequency, phobic avoidance, and anticipatory anxiety.

Some researchers have suggested that repeated infusions of sodium lactate, known to produce terrifying anxiety attacks in panic disorder patients, may habituate these individuals to the panic attack experience (Bonn, Harrison, & Rees, 1973). However, the complexity and potential danger of the lactate infusion procedure renders this approach impractical. Sheehan et al. (1985) anecdotally reports than he has never seen any of his research subjects become desensitized to the lactate challenge test, despite up to four infusions.

In summary, the human service professional seeking a viable psychosocial treatment for clients with panic disorder is offered very few alternatives from the empirical literature. Respiratory control training offers some promise, but other approaches have only anecdotal reports or single-subject experiments to support their use. Traditional psychotherapy, supportive psychotherapy, and hypnosis have not yet been shown to be effective in treating panic disorder.

PHARMACOLOGICAL TREATMENTS FOR PANIC DISORDER

The literature on pharmacological treatments for panic disorder overlaps considerably with that for treating agoraphobics with panic attacks, and as noted earlier, the two diagnoses probably represent polar extremes of the same disorder. The same medications found useful in temporarily alleviating the panic attacks associated with agoraphobia are effective with clients who have panic disorder: the tricyclic antidepressants (Gonzalez, 1982), the monoamine-oxidase inhibitors (Sheehan, 1985), and only one drug of the benzodiazepine family, alprazolam (Chouinard, Annable, Fontaine, & Solyom, 1982; Sheehan, 1985). Other commonly used tranquilizers are of little value in alleviating panic attacks, although they do provide some relief from anticipatory anxiety (McNair & Kahn, 1981; Sheehan, Ballenger, & Jacobson, 1980). The beta-adrenergic compounds such as propranolol do not block panic attacks, but again they may help alleviate the somatic symptoms associated with anticipatory anxiety (Gorman et al., 1982).

The caveats that apply to the drug therapy of agoraphobia apply to the management of panic disorder as well. The return of panic attacks upon discontinuance of these medications is common, as are unpleasant side effects. The antidepressants have the advantage of being nonaddictive, whereas alprazolam, a benzodiazepine, should not be used to treat clients with a history of drug or alcohol abuse. When a decision is made to discontinue drug therapy, the client should be tapered off these compounds very slowly. Abrupt termination of a high-dose regimen of alprazolam has resulted in seizures (Levy, 1984), and isolated instances of maniclike states induced by alprazolam are reported in the literature (Rosenbaum, Woods, Grove, & Klerman, 1984; Strahan, Rosenthal, Kaswan, & Winston, 1985). On the positive side, accidental or intentional overdose with alprazolam appears much less life-threatening than overdose with the tricyclic antidepressants (McCormick, Nielsen, & Jatlow, 1985).

SUMMARY

A further consideration for the human service professional deciding upon treatment options for the client with agoraphobia or panic disorder is the social validity or acceptability of the regimen. Survey experiments of the opinions of the general public and of agoraphobics pertaining to descriptions of exposure therapy, antidepressant medication, tranquilizers, cognitive therapy, or relationship-based treatment found the drug therapies to be the least acceptable alternatives in terms of their likelihood of producing positive short-term benefits or a long-term cure (Norton, Allen, & Hilton, 1983, p. 525). The most highly acceptable psychosocial therapy was therapeutic exposure.

Sociologists have critiqued the inappropriate use of tranquilizers or other drugs by physicians in the care of the anxious patient, for "in doing so, they encourage patients to be dependent on them and their medications, discredit lay advice and help, and generally make little attempt to help them to handle their own lives or to become aware of the links between social structure and ill health" (Gabe & Lipshitz-Phillips, 1984). The human service professional counseling anxious clients must resist the temptation to seek an apparent "quick and easy" cure via medication. At the same time, he or she must be open to the developing empirical research on the pharmacotherapy of anxiety so that when the need arises, treatment or referral of clients for medication can be judiciously employed in appropriate cases.

Chapter 6

OBSESSIVE-COMPULSIVE DISORDER
Assessment and Treatment Strategies

Present fears are less than horrible imaginings.

—Shakespeare, *Macbeth*

Of all the traditional neuroses, obsessive-compulsive disorder (OCD) presents the greatest challenge to the human service professional. Although the first clear description of OCD as a mental disorder was presented by Freud (1909/1955c), it is widely recognized that the "techniques of free association, therapeutic anonymity, transference, dream interpretation, the use of the couch and all the traditional therpeutic techniques" (Salzman, 1966, p. 1139) have been of little value in alleviating compulsive rituals or obsessional ruminations. The current diagnostic criteria for OCD are presented in Table 12, and the clinical features are usually so striking that diagnosis is not often difficult.

Current research has delineated that clients suffering from OCD present with one or more of the following features: (1) compulsive washing; (2) compulsive checking; (3) obsessional thoughts, impulses, or images; and (4) obsessional slowness. Most clients present with some combination of the above symptom clusters, usually multiple rituals and obsessions. The purely obsessional client or individual suffering with obsessional slowness is relatively rare.

Washing rituals may be a function of two distinct factors: a morbid fear of germs or of some other type of unspecified contamination, or as a type of "undoing" or restitutive behavior. Clients with a fear of germs may focus on cleaning their bodies or their environment and may be exceedingly fearful of coming into contact with potential contaminates or, alternatively, of somehow being responsible for contaminating others. Ritualizers in the latter category are often preoccupied with the notion that they will spread their bodily fluids (urine, semen, saliva, menstrual or vaginal secretions) or fecal material.

Checking rituals seem to be designed to forestall some future (usually

Table 12: Diagnostic Criteria for Obsessive Compulsive Disorder

---

A. Either obsessions or compulsions:

Obsessions: recurrent, persistent ideas, thoughts, images, or impulses that are ego-dystonic, i.e., they are not experienced as voluntarily produced but rather as thoughts that invide consciousness and are experienced as senseless or repugnant. Attempts are made to ignore or suppress them.

Compulsions: repetitive and seemingly purposeful behaviors that are performed according to certain rules or in a stereotyped fashion. The behavior is not an end in itself but is designed to produce or prevent some future event or situation. However, either the activity is not connected in a realistic way with what it is designed to produce or prevent, or may be clearly excessive. The act is performed with a sense of subjective compulsion coupled with a desire to resist the compulsion (at least initially). The individual generally recognizes the senselessness of the behavior (this may not be true for young children) and does not derive pleasure from carrying out the activity, although it provides a release of tension.

B. The obsessions or compulsions are a significant source of distress to the individual or interfere with social or role functioning.

C. Not due to another mental disorder, such as Tourette's disorder, schizophrenia, major depression, or organic mental disorder.

SOURCE: American Psychiatric Association (1980, p. 235).

unrealistic) catastrophe, although clients may be unable to explain what it is they fear may occur. Such clients engage in ego-dystonic and stereotypic behavior such as the repetitive checking of locked doors, lights, stoves, or other appliances and water faucets. It is not uncommon for such clients to enclose and reopen their own correspondence repeatedly prior to mailing it, often dozens of times. Variations in these ritualistic behaviors include compulsive counting or touching objects. Repeating certain actions, such as exiting a door or donning a garment, may be continued a certain specified number of times or until it feels "right."

Obsessional thoughts, impulses, and images are subjectively repugnant to the client and are usually associated with themes of guilt, recrimination, or causing violence or injury to others (often loved ones) or with obscene, blasphemous, or sexual content. The client may be concerned that he or she will carry out these morbid ideas or utter bizarre thoughts aloud at inappropriate times. Although this latter situation often does occur (i.e., the client blurts out an obsessional phrase), it is extremely unlikely for the client with OCD to otherwise execute malignant preoccupations. A few examples will illustrate typical themes which preoccupy obsessional clients.

One man in his early 30s was troubled throughout the day with the thought and image of cutting off the penis of his two-and-a-half-year-old son (a sort of reverse Oedipus complex?). A young woman complained of a frequent mental image of a flaming sword descending from a cloud hovering over her head and piercing her side. When given a golf counter and instructed to keep track of the daily frequency of these obsessional images for a one-week period, it was found that they occurred an average of 600 times per day! It is easy to see how such symptoms, although entirely subjective, can incapacitate a client in terms of psychosocial and vocational functioning.

Primary obsessional slowness has only recently been recognized as a rare variant of OCD (Rachman, 1974). Such individuals demonstrate a pathological degree of meticulousness and care in performing relatively unimportant and routine tasks. Toothbrushing or showering may require over an hour of the individual's time, or even longer. In the presence of such clients, one has the sense that time itself has slowed down. Psychomotor retardation is often present as these people go about their tasks, and although some degree of repetition in their actions may be present, as in carefully brushing several teeth over and over again prior to going on to the next group, the dysphoric quality associated with other forms of ritualistic behavior (i.e., washing, checking, touching, counting) is not present. Rather, for these individuals the pace of life has slowed, and they may not subjectively experience any need to speed things along, although spouses and employers may be annoyed with them.

A former OCD client of mine agreed to prepare a detailed written description of her rituals and obsessions. The 18-page, single-spaced, handwritten document was meticulously drafted (not surprisingly) and contained a number of examples of classical obsessive-compulsive symptoms. Below are some representative quotations.

Washing: "I wash my hands five times each time I wash and count to 25 each time I wash. If I cannot wash five times because I am being observed, I wash one time but I feel bad. I dry my hands on a towel counting to 25. If I am in public and can't find a bathroom, I wet my hands in a drinking fountain if I am alone. . . . If I have the front of my clothes wet from drying my hands on them, I touch my hands to them and feel better. . . . I sometimes take a pan of water to my bedroom and put it next to the bed so I can wash and not have to keep getting up. . . . I am afraid if I don't wash that God will think I mean the bad thoughts. I wash to make up for and to prevent them. . . . I have to wash my hands over and over before I leave the house. If I don't do it right, I have to go back in the house and do it again until I feel it is right".

Obsessions: (The client was troubled by blasphemous and obscene thoughts.) "I tell God 'I am sorry,' 'I love you,' 'I don't mean it,' 'I love you very much,' anytime I have bad thoughts, don't do my rituals right, and to prevent thoughts. . . . Sometimes it pops out in public in front of other people. It just comes out and people hear me and think I am weird and look at me funny. . . . I am afraid it will come out in front of other people, but am more afraid of not saying it. . . . It goes on all the time, over and over, and I can't stop it. It keeps me and my mind busy trying to outrun it. I do the same things with my bad thoughts, trying to outrun them, trying not to have them, and to make them go away. I can sometimes feel my bad thoughts coming and sometimes they just come without warning."

Touching and counting: "I do a lot of touching things. I touch my right hand to my breast or leg. I touch things like glasses I am drinking from by touching the glass and retouching it before I drink from it while I count to 11 in my mind . . . . Sometimes I just take one swallow and count fast and sometimes I take 11 little sips, but I always count to 11. I touch my forehead 11 times with my fingers in little taps. I touch furniture with my fingers. I touch the door handle over again and sometimes I touch without counting. . . . I turn on the radio 11 times before I can listen to it and sometimes have to repeat it over again to be able to keep listening."

Checking: "I have always been bothered by looking for my keys and looking to see if I have money, even though I already know I do. I often look to see if they are there. . . . I go through important papers to see if they are still there. I put a lot of old papers and junk in a paper bag to throw them out, but now am afraid to throw it out in case there is something important in it. I will have to go through it again, one piece at a time before I toss it out. . . . Whenever I mail anything out, I always keep putting it in the envelope and taking it out and looking it over. I feel like I might have done something wrong or I left something out. Finally I put it in the envelope and mail it, but worry about it."

This particular client was in her late 30s and had suffered from severe OCD since her mid-20s, following the death of her father. At the time of her referral to the Anxiety Disorders Program she had received psychotherapy for ten years, numerous medications (tranquilizers, antipsychotics, antidepressants), several lengthy hospitalizations, and courses of electroconvulsive therapy. She was unable to hold down a job, although in good physical health, and lived alone, subsisting on a psychiatric disability pension. By no means are all clients with OCD this impaired, but an extreme case of this nature illustrates the potential extent of the handicaps associated with the disorder.

ETIOLOGY AND NATURAL HISTORY

The present state of etiological understanding of OCD is considerably less developed than that for the other anxiety disorders, such as simple and social phobia and agoraphobia. Males and females appear to be equally vulnerable to experiencing OCD, and the average age of onset is about 25 years (Thyer, Parrish, Curtis, Cameron, & Nesse, 1985). A histogram depicting the reported ages of onset for a series of 27 obsessive-compulsives seen at the Anxiety Disorders Program at the University of Michigan Hospitals is presented in Figure 10. Particularly noteworthy is the fact that in over 30% of the cases at onset occurred prior to age 20. This is striking considering the relative dearth of studies on childhood OCD (Flament & Rapoport, 1984). Anecdotally there have been suggestions that OCD tends to run in families, but the relative contributions of family versus genetic influences remain to be isolated. It was shown in one study that stressful life events (illness in the family or self, births, severe arguments, etc.) are over twice as frequent during the 12 months prior to the onset of OCD in the lives of clients with that condition, compared to the lives of individuals in a matched comparison group (McKeon, Roa, & Mann, 1984). An early study reporting that OCD clients scored higher on a questionnaire measure of sensitivity to guilt and criticism than did simple phobics (Turner, Steketee, & Foa, 1979) was held to support certain theories postulating such a dynamic as central and specific to OCD. A replication study involving not only a control group of simple phobics but of social phobics and agoraphobics as well (Thyer, Curtis, & Fechner, 1984) found that these latter two groups were indistinguishable from the OCD patients in terms of their scores on the guilt and criticism measure. Other studies evaluting the role of guilt in OCD have also failed to find the predicted relationship (Manchanda, Sethi, & Gupta, 1979), undermining the notion that OCD is a "guilt neurosis." In general, "the focus on aggression, anger, hostility and similar elements in the essential dynamics of this disorder have not yielded the therapeutic alteration to justify a continued attachment to their validity as etiological factors" (Salzman & Thaler, 1981, p. 291).

Clients with OCD often present with associated psychopathology such as depression, phobias, or panic attacks. The links among these conditions are not clear. Some researchers advocate the position that OCD symptomatology is secondary to associated, primary disorders; others postulate that associated symptoms are the sequelae to the dysphoria and handicaps following the onset of OCD; and a third stance suggests that OCD and other problems may be concurrent yet unrelated

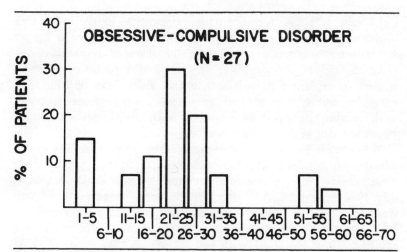

Figure 10. Distribution of the ages of onset (in five-year time periods) for 27 patients with obsessive compulsive disorder. Reprinted from Thyer, Parrish, Curtis, Cameron, and Nesse (1985, p. 119).

(Jenicke, 1983). It is also not clear to what extent the DSM-III Axis II diagnosis of Compulsive Personality Disorder is a precursor or otherwise related to OCD. What has become clear recently is that many of the symptoms associated with OCD occur far more commonly among the general population than has been previously thought. A recent NIMH psychiatric epidemiological study found the incidence of OCD in the general population to be 2%, a figure similar to that found among psychiatric patients. Recent studies have examined the prevalence of intrusive cognitions of an obsessional quality among "normal" individuals (Clark & de Silva, 1985; Rachman & de Silva, 1978; Salkovskis & Harrison, 1984). In one series of 302 individuals sampled, about 84% reported experiencing unpleasant, unwanted thoughts and impulses. Such data suggest that the factors associated with the clinical entity of OCD may represent an exaggeration of experiences common among the general population, as opposed to a unique psychopathological process exclusively associated with patient samples.

Most theorists from a behavioral perspective view overt ritualistic behaviors and "undoing" obsessional thinking as negatively reinforced operant responses. The hypothesized chain of events is that the client experiences either an anxiety-evoking environmental event (e.g., possible germ exposure) or upsetting cognition. His or her learning history has led to the development of ritualistic behaviors that *temporarily* serve to reduce anxiety (e.g., washing, checking, or subvocal speech such as "I don't mean it"). This formulation is supported by extensive research that demonstrates that most compulsive rituals *are* anxiety reducing, yet it does not satisfactorily explain the *development* of dysphoric obsessions themselves. Retrospective appeals to a hypothetical learning history to explain a pathological fear of germs may be intuitively satisfying, but until an adequate empirical base is developed to verify such learning histories in most cases of OCD, behavioral formulations have the status of theory only, not fact.

A few behaviorally oriented researchers have emphasized the role of social contingencies in the client's environment as responsible for the development and maintenance of compulsive rituals (Bailey & Atchinson, 1969; Silverman, 1977). Repeated requests for reassurance ("You don't really think I caught germs just now, do you?") may be inadvertently reinforced by the client's relatives or medical caregivers (Hallam, 1974). Although such operant factors may maintain OCD symptoms, it is difficult to construe how they could result in the development of the disorder, given the intense dysphoric content of obsessions and sense of resistance during the performance of rituals.

Biologically based theories of OCD have received indirect support at best. For example, surgery of the cingulate gyrus or medial frontal lobe produces some symptomatic improvements in severely obsessional patients (Mitchell-Heggs, Kelly, & Richardson, 1976). This has implied to some researchers a form of anatomical pathology as responsible for OCD. Although various symptom clusters associated with OCD are known to be the result of certain neurological disorders (e.g., encephalitis, meningitis, Tourette's syndrome, epilepsy, head trauma), the differences between such patients and the client with OCD are striking enough to render the differential diagnosis easy to make (Cameron, 1985). Although occasional reports of electroencephalographic abnormalities among OCD patients appear in the literature, most reviewers of this research conclude that the EEG is generally normal in nonpsychotic obsessive-compulsives (Jenicke, 1983). Hypothalamic-pituitary-adrenal axis functioning, as measured by the dexamethasone suppression test, distinguishes the OCD patient from the general population (Kerber, Cameron, Curtis, & Thyer, 1986), suggesting some form of neuroendocrine dysfunction in OCD. Until the specific locus of this abnormality is located, however, the finding has little clinical or theoretical import. Studies examining the therapeutic efficacy of various medications in treating OCD will be reviewed below. Although it is often implied by biologically oriented psychiatrists that a disorder's response to a class of pharmacological agents yields insights into the underlying pathophysiology of the disorder, such assertions are clearly premature in the instance of OCD.

CLINICAL MANAGEMENT

Arriving at the DSM-III diagnosis of OCD is only the first step in undertaking the assessment of such patients. Given the heterogeneous nature of the symptom patterns in OCD, careful assessment is required of each aspect of the client's behavior. There are at least three useful global self-report measures designed for use with obsessive-compulsives: the Leyton Obsessionality Inventory (Cooper, 1970), the Sandler-Hazari Obsessionality Inventory (Sandler & Hazari, 1960), and the Maudsley Obsessional-Compulsive Inventory (MOCI; Hodgson & Rachman, 1977). Of these, the MOCI is the best validated, yet easy to administer, consisting of 30 face-valid true-false items. The MOCI has four separately scored components—checking, cleaning, slowness, and doubting—and thus may be used for clients with multiple complaints, as is the usual case. For the purpose of evaluating the effects of treatment, the MOCI could be given monthly, prior to during, and after therapy.

Distinct rituals may be measured in terms of the frequency of each (e.g., how many times each day did the client compulsively wash?) or of their duration (how long did the client spend washing?). Data may be collected by either the client or collaterals. Obsessional thoughts or impulses are most commonly assessed as a frequency measure, and clients may be given golf counters or notebooks to record such data. As might be expected, clients with OCD are often quite cooperative and conscientious about keeping track of their symptoms for the human service professional, once the purpose of gathering such information has been adequately explained.

TREATING COMPULSIVE RITUALS

The treatment of choice in the reduction of compulsive rituals consists of a combination of prolonged exposure to ritual-provoking cues combined with complete response prevention of ritualistic acts, both overt and covert. In many ways the approach is similar to that undertaken in treating the client with exogenous phobias: therapeutic exposure plus persuasion not to flee. The human service professional generally needs to treat separate rituals individually (e.g., washing and counting), as opposed to providing general, nonspecific therapy that exerts an anticompulsive effect.

Careful stimulus mapping should be undertaken to determine accurately the precise cues that provoke ritualizing, and a clinical decision must be made as to where to begin treatment. With the psychologically fragile client or one with few psychosocial resources for support, it may be best to choose one of the less pervasive and demanding rituals, whereas the robust client may tolerate initial efforts focused upon the most debilitating rituals. Treatment may be successfully undertaken in an outpatient setting, particularly if the client's spouse, relatives, or significant others can be properly instructed to assist with his or her care. Inpatient treatment may be required for the client who is grossly incapacitated by rituals or who proves to be a treatment failure on an outpatient basis.

Once a target ritual is jointly agreed upon by the human service professional and client and preliminary stimulus mapping has been completed, a several-hour block of time should be scheduled for the first treatment session. The client needs to be induced to come into contact deliberately with overt ritual-provoking cues, or to think ritual-provoking covert equivalents, and to tolerate the intense anxiety this engenders for a sufficiently long period of time to pass, allowing him or her to calm down. During this habituation period the client must be persuaded to forego *all* ritualistic activities designed to reduce anxiety, otherwise the session will prove less effective.

As an example, for the compulsive hand washer who has a morbid fear of germs, stimulus mapping may reveal that shaking hands with strangers, touching doorknobs of public buildings, and handling money are ritual-provoking cues. A treatment session may involve introducing the client to agency staff (shaking each of their hands), going in and out of doors (with the client handling the doorknobs), and having the client make some purchases (handling the change and paper currency). Once the client has been partially or thoroughly contaminated, a return to the consulting room should follow, with the remainder of the time spent in engaging the client in supportive (but not reassuring) conversation and in assessing his or her level of anxiety (0 = absolutely no compulsion to wash, 100 = an irresistable compulsion to wash). The human service professional must be alert to the client performing surreptitious rituals designed to partially alleviate anxiety (e.g., subtle touching or counting, covert self-reassurance) and encourage the client both to refrain from these actions and to tell you truthfully when they are occurring. Clearly a good therapuetic relationship is an absolute prerequisite for this form of treatment. These sessions should be prolonged until the client can demonstrate calmness and appears capable of refraining from rituals designed to undo the recent contamination. At this stage a cooperative spouse or relative proves useful, in assisting the client with the response prevention elements of treatment when away from the presence of the human service professional. Similarly, a recovered obsessive-compulsive or a support group for anxious clients can serve this monitoring function.

As when working with the phobic client, the human service professional should be aware that this combination of therapeutic exposure and response prevention is a psychologically and physically demanding experience for the client but nonetheless extremely safe for use with healthy individuals. I am aware of no published or unpublished instances of clients experiencing a "psychotic break," outbreak of hysterical panic, or heart attack as a result of this treatment regimen. Indeed, despite relatively intense levels of initial discomfort, most clients habituate (i.e., lose the overwhelming urge to ritualize) anywhere from several minutes to several hours after exposure begins. As in the care of the phobic, longer sessions are more beneficial than short ones, and more frequent sessions are better than sessions spread weeks apart.

Initially one may begin with relatively low levels of exposure to ritual-provoking cues (e.g., asking the client to touch his or her forefinger to a public lavatory door knob), moving in subsequent sessions to "massive" amounts of contamination (e.g., obtaining paper currency and asking the client to rub it on hands, arms, and face). Therapist modeling of such self-exposure is helpful, and it goes without saying that the client should never be asked to perform potentially harmful activities.

Treatment efforts should expand outside of the office setting. A discarded tissue found in the agency's lobby may be just the item for the client to pick up and keep for the next week in purse or wallet. Client hand washing may need to be observed by relatives and strictly limited in time to the dictates of hygiene. The human service professional should instruct the significant others in the client's life not to respond to requests for reassurance from the client pertaining to the safety or harmfulness of the tasks the client is undertaking ("You don't think there are cancer germs on this money, do you?"), giving a neutral response such as "I am not supposed to reassure you," or even better—a response designed to increase the salience of the exposure task ("Why of course there are cancer germs on the money, keep it away from me!"). The use of this latter tactic needs to be carefully explored with the client by the human service professional in advance of its execution.

The typical sequence of events is that most clients can control their ritualistic acts fairly soon, but compulsive urges may persist for quite some time, perhaps for days or weeks. This possibility needs to be anticipated and explained to the client and not viewed as a sign of imminent treatment failure. The rapidity of the decay of compulsive urges seems to be directly proportional to the amount of therapeutic exposure practiced by the client *and* his or her success in response prevention. Occasional "slip-ups" can be tolerated, but the client who goes home from appointments only to engage in massive amounts of ritualizing designed to undo a session's activities is unlikely to make much progress.

After a ritual has been successfully resisted for some time and the client has learned to tolerate exposure to stimuli that formerly provoked rituals, the acute urgency to ritualize will gradually diminish in a manner analogous to that of the alcoholic who has remained sober. The client may need to guard carefully against the reemergence of rituals for weeks or months to come, and booster sessions of exposure and response prevention may be needed periodically. An absolute, complete, and permanent remission of ritualizing symptoms is not common, unfortunately. Occasional brief flare-ups of rituals may be expected, or a reemergence of the subjective urgency to ritualize. However, the above approach has been clearly shown in well-designed controlled clinical trials to be the most effective psychosocial treatment available to help obsessive-compulsive ritualizers regain control over their lives and restore their ability to work and to love (Kirk, 1983).

TREATING OBSESSIONS

The development of effective therapies for the purely obsessional client has lagged behind that of treating the compulsive ritualizer. Neither conventional psychotherapies, behavioral treatment, nor contemporary pharmacological approaches have yet been shown, in rigorous research, to produce specific antiobsessional effects (Marks, 1983a; Rachman & Hodgson, 1980). In part this is due to the relative scarcity of such individuals and also to the ephemeral nature of the disorder. Because obsessions are a purely private event whose controlling variables are difficult to isolate, both clinical intervention and research are rendered somewhat difficult. Because stimulus mapping of the cues that provoke obsessions may prove fruitless, an alternative strategy is to seek to habituate the obsessional client to the specific content of his or her intrusive thoughts, images, or impulses. This may be undertaken in a variety of ways, centered upon the re-creation of obsessional material for prolonged periods of time, thus utilizing this material to undertake therapeutic exposure. This may be done by having the client *write out* in great detail core intrusive thoughts when they occur, *read* such materials for prolonged periods of time, or recite the content of obsessions onto a tape recording and then have the client listen to this material repeatedly. It has been experimentally shown that *prolonged* exposure to obsessional material generally leads to habituation—that is, the material no longer evokes anxiety. A number of single-case reports and small uncontrolled group studies confirm the success of this strategy (Likierman & Rachman, 1982; Salkovskis, 1983; Stambaugh, 1977). The case study described below (abstracted from Thyer, 1985) outlines the management of an obsessional patient.

CASE HISTORY

The client was a 36-year-old white woman who came to the Anxiety Disorders Program complaining of pervasive fears of knives and other sharp objects such as scissors. Careful assessment revealed that the patient met the DSM-III criteria for obsessive-compulsive disorder. Two years earlier she had read a true account of a man who had apparently run amok, murdering a number of people with an axe and then setting fire to his house, wherein he perished. She did not experience an abnormally troubled reaction upon initially reading this story. Several days later the patient was in her daughter's bedroom repairing wall plaster with a sharp putty knife. As she stood over her daughter's bed she recollected the murderous account read earlier and was suddenly seized with a morbid fear that someday she too would go insane and murder her family with a knife. This episode marked the beginning of subsequent daily, repetitive intrusive thoughts and images of a highly disturbing nature, focused upon the theme of her suddenly loosing control of her actions and stabbing her daughter. As a consequence she developed a morbid aversion to the sight or use of knives, and either discarded or hid from view all sharp household implements.

There was an apparent absence of any premorbid obsessive-compulsive symptomatology, psychosis, or impulse control disorder. This pattern of the sudden onset of a full-blown obsession centered upon thoughts of violence, however, has been recognized to occur with relative frequency in the etiology of OCD (Blacker & Levitt, 1979). There was an absence of compulsive rituals such as checking or washing.

COURSE OF TREATMENT

Obsessions are known to be more resistent to treatment than overt compulsive rituals or avoidance behavior (Rachman & Hodgson, 1980).

Therefore, efforts first focused upon helping the client to overcome her fear of knives and other sharp objects through the use of standard real-life exposure therapy (Thyer, 1981, 1983, 1985b). Initially the patient's avoidance of knives was treated in the office, followed by explicit homework assignments for her to conduct independently in her natural environment. She would practice, for example, looking at and handling butcher knives (which were maximally anxiety provoking) in the consulting room, aided by the human service professional's modeling, encouragement, and reassurance. Mutual visits were made to local cutlery shops, where she asked the clerk to let her examine various sharp cutting tools. At home, she was instructed to take all her knives out of the drawer where she had hid them and to keep them stored in a clear glass container on the kitchen countertop. She was asked to resume the practice of cutting her daughter's nails with small scissors and to periodically trim her bangs. In the latter stages of treatment she was instructed to set up situations at home involving butcher knives and her daughter. For example, she would arrange to have the two of them prepare elaborate meals together with sharp knives casually laid on the countertop between them as they worked side by side. Extreme care was taken for the patient to arrange these homework assignments as a part of natural mother-daughter interactions.

Formal treatment sessions were conducted biweekly, and the patient's subjective fears of knives and overt avoidance behavior rapidly decreased during the two months of exposure therapy this entailed. However, obsessional imagery and ideation continued unabated, and she began to complain bitterly about their persistence. Accordingly, therapeutic attention was focused upon the obsessions per se. The patient was asked to write out a complete and detailed account of her intrusive thoughts and not to omit any unpleasant aspects. Previously she had expended a great deal of energy in suppressing her intrusive thoughts and images, and the four-page description she returned with at the next appointment was the first time she had fully faced her obsessional scenario. She rehearsed reading the obsession a few times in front of the human service professional (initially with profuse tears and a tremulous voice) and then dictated it onto an audiocassette tape. Following the lead of Parkinson and Rachman (1980), her instructions were to listen privately to the tape ten consecutive times per day and to record the maximum degree of anxiety she experienced upon hearing each repetition. She was trained in the use of Wolpe's (1969) Subjective Anxiety Scale (0 = complete calmness; 100 = panic or terror) to quantify her obsessional fears. This self-report measure is extensively employed as an outcome measure in clinical research and therapy in the anxiety disorders and is known to be associated with several measures of autonomic arousal (Thyer, Papsdorf, Davis, & Vallecorsa, 1984). Compliance with the above practitioner instigations was enhanced by having the patient read a self-help manual describing the rationale and conduct of exposure therapy (Marks, 1978) and discussing any questions she may have had with the therapist.

RESULTS

Despite the extreme anxiety engendered upon listening to the recorded obsession, the patient reliably practiced her homework assignments. The results from the first 11 weeks of this program are presented in Figure 11. The patient experienced near terror on the first day of homework practice while listening to the ten repetitions of the obsessional tape. Anxiety appeared to decrease little, if any. Nevertheless, clinical improvements became apparent with repeated practice over time, and by the end of 11 weeks she had reached a plateau, consistently reporting anxiety scores of between 0 and 20 points. No further decreases became apparent during weekly practice for an additional two weeks. By the end of the fiftieth day she was complaining that the tape was very boring and it was hard for her to endure listening to a full ten repetitions, not because of anxiety but because of tedium. On day 54, in fact, she quit listening to the tape after eight trials. Of greater clinical significance is that concurrent with the reduction of anxiety reported when listening to the obsessional tape, the patient noted that the frequency of spontaneous obsessional ideation greatly decreased, and that on their rare occurrences they no longer bothered her. At the conclusion of this program the patient was free from intrusive thoughts and comfortable using knives and other sharp objects around her daughter. Written correspondence from the patient 12 months after the termination of treatment indicated continued remission of obsessive-compulsive symptomatology.

SPECIAL CONSIDERATIONS

A number of biological psychiatrists have reported that various pharmacological interventions are valuable in the treatment of the obsessive-compulsive client. The most extensively researched class of compounds used with OCD has been the tricyclic antidepressants (Insel & Murphy, 1981; Marks, Stern, Mawson, Cobb, & McDonald, 1980; Mavissakalian & Michelson, 1983; Mavissakalian, Turner, Michelson, & Jacob, 1985; Thoren, Asberg, Cronholm, Jornestedt, & Traskman,

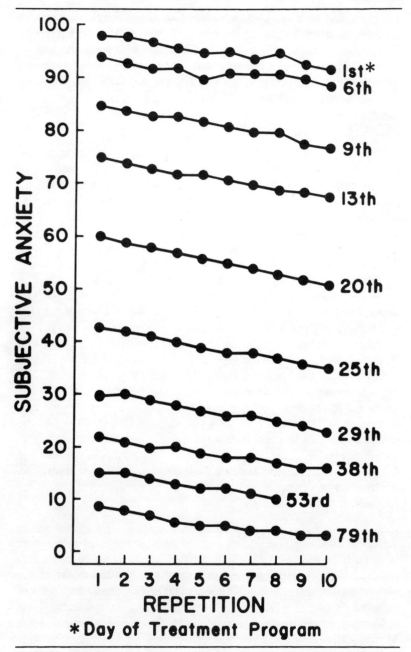

Figure 11. The effects of satiation to obsessive ideation on subjective anxiety in an obessional neurotic. Reprinted from Thyer (1985a, p. 272).

1983), and the most promising of these agents has been clomipramine, a tricyclic antidepressant that is not yet currently approved for use in the United States. Much of this research has produced equivocal findings, and conclusions are often limited because few studies directly measure the frequency or duration of compulsive rituals or obsessions, relying instead upon global rating scales of client dysfunction, which are of dubious validity. Marks (1983a) has extensively reviewed the clinical research literature on the use of purported antiobsessional agents and concluded that such compounds are primarily beneficial for use with patients with concurrent major depression, and that these drugs have antidysphoric effects but are of little value in alleviating rituals or obsessions in nondepressed clients with obsessive-compulsive disorder. Debate on this matter will no doubt continue, but at present there does not appear to be an effective pharmacological regimen that can be recommended as a first-choice treatment for most clients with OCD.

Various forms of psychosurgery have had moderately favorable effects on patients with intractable rituals or obsessions that have failed to respond to more conservative psychosocial therapies or to medication (Bridges, Goktepe, Maratos, Browne, & Young, 1973; Michell-Heggs et al., 1976; Tippin & Henn, 1982), but this option is properly available only through a few highly specialized neurosurgey departments, usually affiliated with university hospital settings.

It has been shown that severely depressed obsessive-compulsives have a less favorable outcome when treated with response prevention and therapeutic exposure than do nondepressed clients (Foa, 1979; Foa, Grayson, & Steketee, 1982; Foa et al., 1983). Such treatment-resistant patients may often benefit from an effective trial of tricyclic anti-depressant therapy then followed by psychosocial treatment as described in this chapter (Foa, Steketee, & Groves, 1979). Another contraindication for therapeutic exposure and response prevention is the situation wherein the client truly believes that his or her rituals forestall some realistic catastrophe. For example, some clients with OCD, when questioned as to the validity of their fears, acknowledge that they really know that they will not be harmed by the supposed germ contamination they dread. In the situation where the client is convinced of the validity of his or her obsessional concerns, the prognosis is somewhat less favorable. Related to this, compulsive checking is often motivated by efforts to forestall some specified or unspecified future catastrophe. Such clients may often benefit from having a further element of exposure therapy added to their treatment regimen, consisting of prolonged imagery and structured rumination to these fearful catastrophic events. For example, if a compulsive client washed himself repeatedly to avoid the possibility that he would spread germs, thus causing an epidemic of some disease and costing the lives of thousands, in addition to response prevention and exposure therapy the human service professional should set up a schedule wherein the client imagines such events occurring and that he was responsible and held to blame for the disaster by society. Such fantasy situations should be repeated over and over for prolonged periods of time until they no longer upset the client. Such sessions should also be given as a form of homework assignment for the client to practice in between sessions. Foa et al. (1980) describe the evidence supporting this adjunctive treatment.

SUMMARY

Considering that in the recent past the treatment of the client with obsessive-compulsive disorder was considered one of the most difficult tasks confronting the clinician and considered by many to be hopeless, and that the long-term prognosis for such clients was dismal (Kringlen, 1965), the availability of a moderately effective psychosocial approach to this previously intractable condition is encouraging for the human service professional charged with caring for such clients. Treatment can be time consuming, but this can often be offset with the therapeutic contributions of significant others in the client's life. No doubt the next few decades will continue to bring further positive developments for the relief of handicapping obsessions and rituals.

Chapter 7

GENERALIZED ANXIETY DISORDER
Assessment and Treatment Strategies

What I am to fear I know not
yet none the less I fear all things.

— *Ovid*

Generalized anxiety disorder (GAD) is a new diagnostic label that first appeared in the psychiatric nomenclature with the advent of the DSM-III in 1980. The category of GAD is derived from the earlier term "anxiety neurosis" found in the DSM-II. With the recognition of panic disorder as a discrete diagnostic entity, anxiety neurosis was subdivided into two presumably more precise diagnoses: GAD and panic disorder. Panic disorder has been described in Chapter 4, and to gain an idea of the experience of GAD, imagine the following scenario: It is 10:00 a.m. and you have just finished your twelfth cup of coffee for that morning. You are jittery and tense, unable to concentrate, and feel quite apprehensive and a bit nauseated. In addition, your left eyelid has developed an uncontrollable twitch. The individual suffering from GAD may have felt this way, more or less continuously, for months at a time.

Discussion of GAD requires the introduction of a further category of pathological anxiety. Recall in previous chapters the various types of anxiety that were outlined:

Phobic Anxiety—experienced by individuals directly confronting or exposed to their phobic anxiety-evoking stimulus

Anticipatory Anxiety—experienced by phobic individuals anticipating imminent or delayed exposure to phobic situations, *or* by panic disorder sufferers dreading the next occurrence of spontaneous panic

Panic Anxiety—the abrupt onset of severe fear that catches the individual by surprise, often so intense that the individual believes that he or she is dying or going crazy, yet is apparently *not* evoked by known environmental events or cognitions

In the case of GAD we again have the situation wherein there are no known anxiety-evoking stimuli, yet the individual feels moderately anxious most of the time. This fourth form of pathological anxiety may be termed *generalized anxiety*. The phenomenology of this disorder is almost entirely subjective, with only a few overt behavioral indices. The diagnostic criteria for GAD are listed in Table 13.

There are over 40 possible symptoms that can contribute to the diagnosis, divided into four broad categories: (1) motor tension, (2) autonomic reactivity, (3) apprehensive expectation, and (4) vigilance and scanning. In order for the formal diagnosis of GAD to be made, the individual must experience at least one symptom from at least three of these categories. Moreover, the anxious mood must have persisted more or less continuously for at least one month and not be secondary to another mental disorder.

A sense of the subjective experiences of clients with GAD may be gathered by asking them to rate the intensity of the various symptoms to which they may be subject. Table 14 displays such a list, obtained from 12 patients with GAD seen at the Anxiety Disorders Program and reported by Cameron, Thyer, Nesse, and Curtis (1986). These patients reportedly suffered from GAD for an average of 14.2 years prior to being seen at our clinic. The pattern in the ages of onset is displayed in Figure 12 and indicates that the mean age of onset for this disorder is 22.8 years (s.d. = 12.0). The gender distribution for this sample of patients was 44% female, 56% male. Note that GAD rarely develops in clients older than their mid-30s and that a significant percentage (approximately 40%) report the onset of generalized anxiety before age 20. In the case of a client younger than age 18, the diagnosis of GAD is not allowable according to the DSM-III; the most probable diagnosis would be overanxious disorder.

ASSESSMENT STRATEGIES

Given the difficulties in sorting through this list of possible symptoms during a diagnostic interview with an anxious client, the Anxiety Disorders Program at the University of Michigan Hospitals developed a diagnostic checklist that the human service professional can employ in assessing the client with possible GAD. We had the client complete this checklist prior to our initial interview and at that time the clinician would review the symptoms and criteria with the client to ensure that he or she understood the meaning of the terms and had given accurate answers (see Table 15). After the symptom list is clarified the next step is

Table 13:   Diagnostic Criteria for Generalized Anxiety Disorder

A. Generalized, persistent anxiety is manifested by symptoms from three of the following four categories:
  1. *Motor tension:* shakiness, jitteriness, jumpiness, trembling, tension, muscle aches, fatigability, inability to relax, eyelid twitch, furrowed brow, strained face, fidgeting, restlessness, easy startle.
  2. *Autonomic hyperactivity:* sweating, heart pounding or racing, cold, clammy hands, dry mouth, dizziness, light-headedness, tingling in hands or feet, upset stomach, hot or cold spells, frequent urination, diarrhea, discomfort in the pit of the stomach, lump in the throat, flushing, pallor, high resting pulse and respiration rate.
  3. *Apprehensive expectation:* anxiety, worry, fear, rumination, and anticipation of misfortune to self or others.
  4. *Vigilance and scanning:* hyperattentiveness, resulting in distractability, difficulty in concentrating, insomnia, feeling "on edge," irritability, impatience.

B. The anxious mood has been continuous for at least one month.

C. Not due to another mental disorder, such as depressive disorder or schizophrenia.

D. At least 18 years of age.

SOURCE: American Psychiatric Association (1980, p. 233).

Table 14: Mean Symptom Rankings Reported by Patients
          with Generalized Anxiety Disorder

Rank	Symptom	Mean Score*
1	Difficulty concentrating	3.58
2	Difficulty working	3.50
3	Confusion	3.17
4	Palpitations	2.82
5	Difficulty speaking	2.75
6	Twitching	2.64
7	Feeling of doom	2.55
8	Sweating	2.45
9	Breathing changes	2.42
10	Urge to defecate	2.40
11	Nausea	2.36
12	Sense of unreality	2.27
13	Dizziness	2.26
14	Fear of dying	2.25
15	Urge to urinate	2.18
16	Feeling detached	1.91
17	Feeling faint	1.75

SOURCE: Cameron, Thyer, Nesse, and Curtis (1986).
*Range of possible scores for each item: 1 = none, 2 = mild, 3 = moderate, 4 = severe.

to confirm the duration criteria (fairly continuous symptoms for at least one month). It is highly recommended that the human service professional employ this diagnostic aid, or something similar, in order to prevent the evaluation deteriorating into a series of disjointed questions,

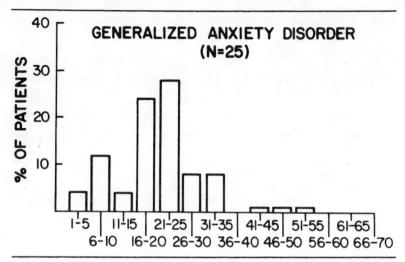

Figure 12. Distribution of ages of onset (in five-year time periods) for 25 patients with generalized anxiety disorder. From Thyer, Parrish, Curtis, Cameron, and Nesse (1985, p. 120).

and to avoid omitting important aspects of the diagnostic interview.

Once the human service professional has confirmed that the client does indeed meet the criteria for a diagnosis of generalized anxiety disorder, the next important task is that of differential diagnosis, systematically excluding alternative biological or mental conditions that may mimic the symptoms of GAD. This is absolutely essential in order to preclude inappropriate treatments. Cameron (1985) reviews the major issues in the differential diagnosis of GAD and notes that most clients presenting with presumptive GAD possess additional symptomatic features that allow for a more specific diagnosis. For example, many clients with panic disorder develop pervasive and fairly continuous anticipatory anxiety, being in a state of more or less constant dread of the next attack of spontaneous panic. If an individual has not had such spontaneous panic attacks for several months it is easy for the human service professional to erroneously diagnose him or her as experiencing GAD. This is incorrect because the diagnosis of panic disorder always supersedes a diagnosis of GAD. In fact, almost every possible differential diagnosis supercedes that of GAD, leading some investigators to conclude that instances of "pure" generalized anxiety are relatively rare in the general or psychiatric population (Cameron, 1985; Klein, Gittelman, Quitkin, & Rifkin, 1980). Individuals with phobias to many different situations, as in agoraphobia, or of stimuli that are fairly

Table 15:   Clinician's Guide to Assessing Generalized Anxiety
                   Disorder Symptomatology*

Name of Patient: _____ Date: _____

In the space provided below, please check "Yes" or "No" indicating which of the
listed sensations or experiences you have fairly constantly, or much of time, day in
and day out.

	Yes	No	Do not write in this space ((Clinician Notes)
Shaky	___	___	
Jittery	___	___	
Jumpy	___	___	
Trembling	___	___	
Tension	___	___	
Muscle aches	___	___	
Tired	___	___	
Can't relax	___	___	
Twitchy eyelids	___	___	
Furrowed brow	___	___	
Strained face	___	___	
Fidgeting	___	___	
Restless	___	___	
Easy to startle	___	___	A.1 ___
Sweating	___	___	
Heart pounding or racing	___	___	
Cold or clammy hands	___	___	
Dry mouth	___	___	
Dizzy	___	___	
Lightheaded	___	___	
Tingling in hands or feet	___	___	
Upset stomach	___	___	
Hot or cold spells	___	___	
Frequent urination	___	___	
Diarrhea	___	___	
Discomfort in pit of stomach	___	___	
Lump in the throat	___	___	
Flushed face	___	___	
Appearing pale	___	___	
Fast heartbeat	___	___	
Fast breathing	___	___	A.2 ___

Table 15:   Continued

	Yes	No	Do not write in this space (Clinician Notes)
Anxiety	___	___	
Worry	___	___	
Fear	___	___	
Dwelling on thoughts	___	___	
Anticipating misfortune (to yourself or others)	___	___	A.3 ___
Easily distracted	___	___	
Hard to concentrate	___	___	
Sleeping poorly	___	___	
Feeling "on edge"	___	___	
Irritable	___	___	
Impatient	___	___	A.4 ___

Feelings like those listed above often come and go or fluctuate quite a bit. Allowing for this, if you have been having these sorts of feelings, how long would you say that it has been since you began having these feelings fairly persistently? Please put down the approximate date, giving a month and year.

I have felt this way fairly persistently since:

*Developed by George C. Curtis, M.D., Anxiety Disorders Program, Department of Psychiatry, The University of Michigan Hospitals, Ann Arbor, MI. Reproduced with permission.

pervasive in their lives, such as the socially phobic client or the obsessive-compulsive with a marked fear of germs, may also display the symptomatic features of GAD, but again the appropriate diagnosis is either agoraphobia, simple or social phobia, or obsessive-compulsive disorder, respectively.

If the development of GAD appears to follow a significant change in the individual's life, such as separation loss (e.g., death of a loved one or moving away from home) or other possible stressor (marriage, divorce, giving birth, taking a new job, etc.), then the appropriate diagnosis is most likely "adjustment disorder with anxious mood." Likewise, if the onset of generalized anxiety follows a clearly traumatic event (e.g., rape or other assault, military combat, severe accidents, or a natural catastrophe), then a diagnosis of "posttraumatic stress disorder" would supersede a diagnosis of GAD.

Another important exclusionary factor is the client's use of drugs that have anxietylike effects. Prime candidates here are the excessive use of caffeine-containing foods or beverages, stimulant compounds (e.g., amphetamines, phenylproponolamine), or binging on foods high in sugar.

There are a large number of biological disorders that have associated anxietylike symptomatology (see Cameron, 1985); conditions such as hyperthyroidism, organic mental disorders, hypoglycemia, pituitary disorders, and neurologic disease are among the most commonly cited. Referral to an appropriate medical specialist such as an endocrinologist or neurologist is always indicated when suspected biological conditions may be contributing to the symptoms associated with GAD. Referral to a psychiatrist per se may not always be helpful because most psychiatrists do not perform physical examinations (McIntyre & Romano, 1977); indeed, a significant percentage do not feel competent to perform physical exams.

The much maligned hyperventilation syndrome is often suggested as a likely differential diagnosis in cases of presumptive GAD, but here we have the question of which is the primary phenomenon—hyperventilation producing anxiety or generalized anxiety resulting in chronic hyperventilation. It is known that anxious individuals hyperventilate and that individuals who hyperventilate can become quite anxious (Thyer, Papsdorf, & Wright, 1984). As in distinguishing suspected panic disorder from hyperventilation syndrome, a hyperventilation challenge test (see Chapter 3) may prove useful. In general, however, most clients with GAD do not rank hyperventilatory phenomena high on their list of subjective experiences (see Table 14), and I suspect that hyperventilation syndrome can be only rarely implicated as a primary cause of GAD.

To summarize, let us review what generalized anxiety disorder is *not*. It is not a reaction to life stress or trauma, nor is it due to drug use or other biological factors. When an individual has a concurrent mental disorder that may give rise to the symptoms of GAD, the appropriate diagnosis is not GAD but rather the associated mental disorder, most commonly panic disorder, agoraphobia, simple or social phobia, obsessive-compulsive disorder, adjustment disorder with anxious mood, posttraumatic stress disorder, "anxious depression," or schizophrenia. Finally, GAD has not yet been shown to be caused by chronic hyperventilation. This leaves us with the perplexing question, "What is generalized anxiety disorder?"

Biological psychiatrists (Sheehan & Sheehan, 1982b; Tallman, Paul, Skolnick, & Gallagher, 1980) postulate that GAD is a metabolic disorder, a biochemical abnormality of the brain. Good evidence in support of this position remains to be established. Familial studies of patients with GAD do not suggest that the condition has a genetic component (Crowe et al., 1983; Torgersen, 1983), and no definitive biological markers have been isolated that clearly identify the client with GAD from other individuals (Hoehn-Saric & McLeod, 1985).

Behaviorally oriented researchers (Wolpe, 1958, 1964) have suggested that cases of "free-floating" anxiety emerge when individuals have developed aversive conditioned emotional reactions to more or less pervasive elements occurring in their environment. In other words, GAD is a more complex form of phobic disorder, the difference being that the anxiety-evoking stimuli are less clear-cut or salient. Examples of such possible amorphous anxiety-evoking cues would be contrasts between light and shade, ambiguous noise, verticality or spatiality, intestinal motility, or simply the passage of time. Wolpe (1964) contends that a failure to isolate these anxiety-evoking stimuli represents either a lack of skill or care on the part of the human service professional or the existence of an underlying organic basis for the chronic anxiousness. According to Wolpe, then, the condition defined by the DSM-III as GAD does not exist—all such apparent cases represent either complex phobic states or a biological disorder. Such a position affords little comfort to the human service professional faced with individuals experiencing generalized anxiety for whom biological factors have been excluded and specific anxiety-evoking stimuli cannot be isolated.

According to psychoanalytic theory, there are two major intrapsychic mechanisms at work giving rise to pathological anxiety. The phenomenon of panic attacks was explained as a partial orgasmic experience, spasmotically erupting and venting forth libidinal energy (Freud, 1924). The more pervasive aspects of apprehension associated with anxiety neurosis were held to be attributable to "signal anxiety," wherein anxiousness indicated to the ego that a repressed wish was threatening to emerge and that severe consequences would follow if this wish were not adequately repressed (Freud, 1962). These two views of anxiety—discharge theory and signal theory—were never fully reconciled. Empirical evidence in support of either view has not appeared, apart from the detailed case histories so favored by the psychoanalytically inclined. In any event, outcome studies of anxious clients treated with conventional psychodynamic therapies have not been encourging (Miles, Barabee, & Finesinger, 1961). To be fair, much of this literature involved the treatment of clients seen prior to 1980 and diagnosed as suffering from anxiety neurosis or an anxiety state, thus presumably mixing clients we would now label as GAD or panic disorder. I am not aware of any outcome studies conducted since 1980 that evaluated the effects of psychotherapy on clients with generalized anxiety disorder;

thus the merits of such treatment approaches may not yet be empirically rejected or embraced.

As of yet no good theory has emerged that accounts for the etiology and maintenance of generalized anxiety disorder. In part this may be due to the relative newness of the diagnostic criteria for the disorder and in part to disagreement as to its very existence. For example, European clinical researchers doubt the reality of pure GAD, generally preferring to retain the old classification system of anxious neurosis (Jablensky, 1985; Tyrer, 1984).

The human service professional faced with evaluating the outcomes of therapy with clients suffering from GAD may choose from a set of self-report scales that purport to measure generalized anxiety. Reliance upon client self-report is required when evaluating outcomes in clients with GAD given the almost entirely subjective aspects of the problem. These scales may be repeatedly completed by the client prior to, during, and after therapy and scored and graphed by the human service professional to obtain a visual depiction of the outcomes of treatment. Such information should, of course, be supplemented by the client's own reports and the human service professional's clinical observations; no self-report scale is capable of capturing *all* aspects of a client's problem (Hudson & Thyer, 1986).

Among the more commonly employed self-report scales are the Spielberger State-Trait Anxiety Inventory (STAI; Spielberger, Gorsuch & Lushene, 1970) and the Zung Anxiety Scale (Zung, 1971). The drawback to these instruments is that they were developed prior to the advent of the DSM-III and thus may not be completely appropriate for use with clients assessed using the current diagnostic nomenclature. My colleagues and I at the School of Social Work at Florida State University recently developed a Clinical Anxiety Scale (CAS) for use in evaluating the outcomes of treatment with clients experiencing pathological anxiety. The CAS was derived in large part from the diagnostic criteria found for the anxiety disorders listed in the DSM-III and is designed to be compatible in format with Hudson's (1982) Clinical Measurement Package, a system of nine self-report scales, similarly formatted and scored, that assess common problems treated by social workers and other human service professionals (e.g., depression, marital conflict, family dysfunction, poor self-esteem, etc.).

The Clinical Anxiety Scale (see Table 16) consists of 25 items which the client is asked to rate on a scale of 1 to 5. The instrument is scored by summing the individual's score on all 25 items (reverse scoring the items marked with an asterisk). Our initial validation study based upon 47

Table 16:   Thyer Clinical Anxiety Score for Use in Evaluating Practice

Clinical Anxiety Scale

Name: _____   Today's Date: _____

This questionnaire is designed to measure how much anxiety you are currently feeling. It is not a test so there are no right or wrong answers. Answer each item as carefully and as accurately as you can by placing a number beside each one as follows:

1 = Rarely or none of the time
2 = A little of the time
3 = Some of the time
4 = A good part of the time
5 = Most or all of the time

Please begin.

1.* I feel calm . . . . 1.——
2. I feel tense. . . . . ·——
3. I feel suddenly scared for no reason . . . . ·——
4. I feel nervous . . . . ·——
5.* I feel confident about the future . . . . ·——
6.* I am free from senseless or unpleasant thoughts . . . . ·——
7. I feel afraid to go out of my house alone . . . . ·——
8.* I feel relaxed and in control of myself . . . . ·——
9. I feel nervousness or shakiness inside . . . . ·——
10. I use tranquilizers or antidepressants to cope with my anxiety . . . . ·——
11. I have spells of terror or panic . . . . ·——
12. I feel afraid in open spaces or in the streets . . . . ·——
13. I feel afraid I will faint in public . . . . ·——
14.* I am comfortable traveling on buses, subways, or trains . . . . ·——
15.* I feel comfortable in crowds, such as shopping or at a movie . . . . ·——
16.* I feel comfortable when I am left alone . . . . ·——
17.* I rarely feel afraid without good reason . . . . ·——
18. Due to my fears, I unreasonably avoid certain animals, objects, or situations ——
19. I get upset easily or feel panicky unexpectedly . . . . ·——
20. My hands, arms, or legs shake or tremble . . . . ·——
21. Due to my fears, I avoid being alone, whenever possible. . . . . ·——
22. Due to my fears, I avoid social situations whenever possible . . . . ·——
23. I experience sudden attacks of panic which catch me by surprise. . . . . . . ·——
24. I feel generally anxious . . . . ·——
25. I am bothered by dizzy spells . . . . ·——

*Items marked with an asterisk are reverse scored. See text for scoring instructions.

clinically anxious individuals and 156 "normals" demonstrated a coefficient alpha for the CAS of .94, reflecting excellent reliability (Westhius, Thyer, & Hudson, 1986). The discriminant validity coefficient was .77, indicating that the CAS is a reasonably valid instrument. A clinical cutting score of 30 was found to minimize the sum of false positives and false negatives. This indicates that, roughly speaking, individuals suffering from pathological anxiety would be likely to score higher than 30 on the CAS, whereas individuals without significant problems due to anxiety would most likely score below 30 points. A human service professional could employ the CAS to monitor a client's level of generalized anxiety throughout the course of treatment. Effective therapy would presumably be reflected in a lowering of CAS scores over time.

TREATMENT STRATEGIES

PHARMACOTHERAPY

Most clients with GAD are initially seen by their personal physician. In fact, anxiety neurosis is the most common mental disorder seen by family practitioners in Great Britain (Dunn, 1983) and the United States. Accordingly, apart from general reassurance, the most common treatment for the anxious individual consists of antianxiety medication, usually one of the benzodiazepine family of drugs. In 1977, 54 million prescriptions were written for diazepam (National Academy of Sciences, 1979), the most widely used tranquilizer. Tallman et al. (1980) conservatively estimated that at least 8000 tons of benzodiazepines were consumed in the United States in 1977. These statistics are all the more striking in light of the fact that as recently as 1978, a review of the double-blind outcome studies (Solomon & Hart, 1978) evaluating the efficacy of the benzodiazepines concluded that "almost all the studies have major flaws in design or execution. Because none of the 78 published double-blind studies on benzodiazepines are fully adequate, and many are so poorly designed and executed as to be meaningless, the efficacy of the entire group of drugs as antianxiety agents must be questioned" (p. 828) and that "the value of any of the benzodiazepines over any of the psychotherapies has yet to be demonstrated" (p. 829).

Nevertheless, benzodiazepine therapy remains the first choice treatment for GAD among biological psychiatrists. There do not appear to be any indications to prefer one over another, although the second-generation benzodiazepine alprazolam has a more favorable sedation/anxiolytic ratio (Elie & Lamontagne, 1984). The major source of debate over the use of benzodiazepines concerns their possible side effects, the possibility of withdrawal symptoms upon discontinuance of the drugs, and the necessary length of time for treatment. Rickels, Case, Downing, & Winokur (1983) recently conducted a well-controlled double-blind clinical outcome study of long-term diazepam therapy of clients with generalized anxiety disorder or atypical anxiety disorder and found some encouraging results. Relatively short-term use of diazepam (i.e., less than eight months) produced an incidence of drug withdrawal symptoms of 5% upon drug discontinuance. Tolerance rarely developed, and, most important, it was found that 50% of the patients treated with diazepam for only six weeks maintained their improvements for an additional 18 weeks (the total study period). The other 50% required more prolonged drug therapy. These results support a fairly conservative approach to the treatment of GAD with benzodiazepines—relatively short-term use, followed by a slow tapering off of the drug, followed by a drug "holiday" period to assess long-term benefits. One cannot deny the risks of abuse or addiction associated with these compounds, but on balance their benefits outweigh their disadvantages. It is clear, however, that the long-term use of benzodiazepine compounds is best avoided.

For clients with a history of drug (e.g., alcohol, benzodiazepines, barbiturates, opiates) abuse, the human service professional should encourage the use of nonaddictive antianxiety compounds. These are reviewed by Hoehn-Saric and McLeod (1985) and include the beta-adrenergic blockers such as propranolol (Noyes, 1985), the antihistaminics (Rickels, 1983), and a newly developed agent, buspirone (Rickels et al., 1982), whose mechanism of action is unknown. Each of these classes of drugs has its own strengths and limitations, requiring careful management by a psychiatrist skilled in the psychopharmacological treatment of anxiety.

PSYCHOSOCIAL TREATMENTS

The nonmedical human service professional may take a number of psychosocial approaches to the care of the client with generalized anxiety disorder. Unfortunately, given the relative newness of the diagnosis, little well-controlled research exists that has evaluated the merits of these approaches. In general, psychosocial therapies to treat GAD fall into one of the following categories: (1) systematic desensitization, (2) progressive muscular relaxation training, (3) biofeedback-assisted relaxation training, (4) meditation, (5) cognitive behavior therapy, and (6) some combination of the above interventions. Caution is indicated in interpreting the clinical literature on these approaches because most of these studies involved the treatment of clients not diagnosed as GAD using contemporary criteria. Most involved therapy of clients with anxiety neurosis, some other ill-defined anxiety state, or a more circumscribed phobic disorder.

Systematic Desensitization

As noted earlier, the founder of systematic desensitization contends that true cases of generalized anxiety disorder do not exist (Wolpe, 1964). In the cases of pervasive anxiety that he has treated, Wolpe claims that meticulous assessment by the human service professional is able to uncover subtle anxiety-evoking cues. Of course, when these are revealed, the practitioner can then undertake conventional systematic desensitization therapy, pairing some response that inhibits anxiety (relaxation, assertiveness, short-acting muscular relaxants) with exposure in fantasy to these anxiety-evoking stimuli. Wolpe (1964) claims, with some crude measures of outcome, that cases of apparent pervasive anxiety can be effectively treated using conventional systematic desensitization, although the mean number of treatment sessions may be four times that required for the successful treatment of less complex neuroses. More recently, Wolpe, Brady, Sarber, Agras, & Liberman (1973) acknowledged that "individuals who are not able to clearly define the what, where and when of their fears are not likely to benefit from systematic desensitization" (p. 962). Thus unless the human service professional can successfully isolate a GAD client's anxiety-evoking stimuli, systematic desensitization or another procedure based upon therapeutic exposure is likely to be of little value.

Relaxation Training

Progressive muscular relaxation training (PMRT) is a nonspecific treatment procedure that is clearly effective in helping individuals develop the capacity to experience profound muscular relaxation, which reduces subjective anxiety and decreases physiological hyperactivity (Bernstein & Borkovec, 1973). The typical course of this treatment involves a number of sessions conducted in the consulting room by the human service professional, perhaps followed by audiotapes that the client is asked to play for the purposes of home-based practice. Some clinical researchers attempt to enable clients to develop their own abbreviated versions of PMRT, following the attainment of good skills at relaxing using the standard format (which typically involves 20-30 minutes of practice alternating tensing and relaxing various muscle groups). Abbreviated self-relaxation is taught in an attempt to enhance the maintenance and generalization of the benefits of relaxation outside the home or clinic setting.

Although the research on the benefits of PMRT is clear in pointing out the positive effects of the procedure, a number of limitations have not been resolved. Virtually no research has been conducted evaluating PMRT in the treatment of clients with generalized anxiety disorder, as defined by the DSM-III. One must extrapolate, a dubious process at best, from research on more circumscribed conditions such as public speaking or test anxiety (Himle, Thyer, Papsdorf, & Caldwell, 1984; Thyer, Papsdorf, Himle, et al., 1981) to the more disabling diagnosis of GAD. A second problem is that home practice on the part of clients is difficult to verify. One recent study showed that clients exaggerated their home practice of PMRT by an average of 126% above their actual efforts, and that only 25% of the clients performed PMRT on a daily basis, despite instructions to do so (Hoelscher, Lichstein, & Rosenthal, 1984). In the absence of daily practice, the benefits of PMRT may be presumed to be appreciably less. A third problem is that a significant minority of clients undergoing PMRT experience a paradoxical transient increase in anxiety during relaxation (Heide & Borkovec, 1984). These instances of relaxation-induced anxiety may be so bothersome as to force some clients to drop out of therapy. Given this final caveat, it is important for the human service professional to proceed cautiously with the implementation of PMRT for the client with GAD and not to assume blithely that the procedure is completely benign.

The primary indication for advocating relaxation training to treat clients with generalized anxiety disorder seems to be the intuitive belief that such individuals stand to benefit from learning to relax. The human service professional may elect to offer such therapy based upon this perspective but should be aware that the empirical evidence supporting such an approach with clients suffering from GAD is meager.

Biofeedback-Assisted Relaxation Training

Much of the enthusiasm for biofeedback as a panacea for psychological ailments that characterized the 1970s has died down. A good deal of this literature related to the treatment of disorders presumably characterized by chronic anxiety or tension (e.g., insomnia, muscle-contraction headaches, anxiety neurosis). The rationale here is that the biofeedback intervention, it was hoped, could facilitate the client's acquisition of the ability to relax deeply. Biofeedback was typically provided of some physiological parameter presumably reflective of general arousal or anxiety—most often frontal area electromyographic activity, heart rate, skin temperature, or electrodermal activity.

Regrettably, no studies have yet been published evaluating the sole use of biofeedback as a treatment for clients with generalized anxiety disorder. A recent critical review of the uses of clinical biofeedback in counseling, psychotherapy, and behavioral medicine concluded, "There is absolutely no convincing evidence that biofeedback is an essential or specific treatment for treating any condition" (Roberts, 1985, p. 940). As practiced today, biofeedback is typically employed as only one clinical tool among an armamentarium of therapeutic practices. The human service professional planning the treatment of clients with generalized anxiety disorder should be skilled in a variety of psychosocial interventions and not attempt to utilize biofeedback-assisted relaxation training as a solitary procedure.

Meditation

A thorough search of the literature did not uncover any reports of the use of meditation as a therapy for clients with generalized anxiety disorder. The human service professional should view such approaches with a skeptical eye. Holmes (1984) exhaustively reviewed all published reports evaluating various types of meditation as a method for reducing somatic arousal, including such responses as heart rate, respiration, electrodermal activity, blood pressure, skin temperature, EMG activity, and metabolic actions. He concluded,

> This review of the published experimental research on the influence of meditation on somatic arousal did not reveal any evidence that meditating subjects attained lower levels of somatic arousal than did resting subjects. Furthermore, the review did not reveal any evidence that subjects who had meditated had less somatic arousal to stressful situations than did subjects who had not meditated. (Holmes, 1984, p. 8)

This is not to say that meditation is not beneficial, only that similar benefits may be obtained by having subjects simply rest for comparable periods of time. Accordingly, the human service professional would be ill-advised to suggest that clients with generalized anxiety disorder invest significant resources of time or money to acquire specific skills in meditation.

Cognitive Behavior Therapy

The premise behind cognitive behavior therapy approaches to the etiology and treatment of generalized anxiety is that chronic anxiety is in part a function of "counterproductive cognitive patterns, unrealistic goals, unreasonable values, assumptions or imperatives learned from significant others" (Beck & Emery, 1985, p. 83). There are some correlational data in support of this position. I and my colleagues (Thyer & Papsdorf, 1981; Himle, Thyer, & Papsdorf, 1982; Thyer, Papsdorf, & Kilgore, 1983) have found statistically significant correlations between self-reported adherence to irrational beliefs and measures of trait of general anxiety. In contrast, the association between irrational thinking and specific fears is very small and has little clinical meaning (Thyer, Papsdorf, & Kramer, 1983). Yet convincing evidence that cognitions *cause* anxiety, and are not merely associated with the phenomenon, has not been forthcoming.

According to Aaron Beck, one of the most influential of the cognitive behavior therapists, the diagnosis of generalized anxiety disorder is actually a misnomer. Similar to Wolpe (1964), Beck believes that with a careful "cognitive analysis" the human service professional is able to pinpoint specific situations that evoke pervasive anxiety and isolate the maladaptive self-statements that clients are telling themselves and that exacerbate anxiety (Beck & Emery, 1985, pp. 94-95). Beck believes that social or interpersonal anxiety is the cornerstone for most cases of apparent generalized anxiety disorder.

Clinical interventions based upon the principles of cognitive behavior therapy usually involve educating the client in how to challenge irrational beliefs on an intellectual level, and/or how to substitute adaptive, positive self-statements for maladaptive ones. Unfortunately, the majority of reports on cognitive behavior therapy for anxiety disorders employ analogue subjects (typically college student volunteers), not actual patients with a diagnosed anxiety disorder. A rare clinical trial involving diagnosed patients (agoraphobics) was conducted by Emmelkamp et al. (1978) and compared the relative efficacy of cognitive behavior therapy versus real-life therapeutic exposure. Therapeutic exposure was found to be a superior form of treatment.

Ramm, Marks, Yuksel, and Stern (1981) treated two groups of six patients diagnosed as suffering from an anxiety state with cognitive behavior therapy, comparing training patients in the use of positive self-statements to cope with anxiety (i.e., "I can cope with these feelings") versus the use of negative self-statements (i.e., "I am really going crazy"). Ramm et al. construed this as a partial test of the proposition that maladaptive cognitions can exacerbate anxiety and that one can obtain therapeutic benefits from altering one's cognitions. Few gains were noted in members of either group, and the overall results were not clinically impressive. Ramm et al. tended to attribute the small positive trend to nonspecific treatment influences. The results did not support the premises of the cognitive behavior therapists. An additional confound is that 10 of the 12 patients suffered from concurrent panic attacks, hence their similarity to patients with GAD is limited.

I was able to locate only one study evaluating the effects of cognitive behavior therapy on clients with GAD. Woodward and Jones (1980) assigned 27 patients with general anxiety to either cognitive behavior therapy (n = 7), systematic desensitization (n = 7), cognitive behavior therapy *plus* systematic desensitization (n = 6), or to no treatment (n = 7). It was found that the combined treatment group was superior to each of the other treatments in isolation on one of eight outcome measures, in addition, the combined treatment was superior to cognitive behavior therapy alone on one of the eight outcome measures. The authors found, in general, that the cognitive therapy failed to produce any significant clinical improvements in their patients, leading them to speculate that cognitive restructuring interventions may work better with the typical analogue population of college students that with psychiatric patients from the general population.

Combination Interventions

The earliest of these combination interventions is a general report by Cautela (1966) containing a description of his approach to the treatment of pervasive anxiety, along with three case histories. Cautela offered his patients the following package of interventions:

(1) Reassurance therapy—letting the patient know that the human service professional is available at *all* times. This involves taking calls at odd hours or having patients drop by unannounced. Generally, Cautela notes, after the client "tests" the human service professional a few times these calls and visits become rare but that clients find this option very reassuring.

(2) Systematic desensitization in fantasy—dependent, of course, on the human service professional being able to isolate specific anxiety-evoking stimuli.

(3) Progressive muscular relaxation training, couples with self-statements pertaining to calmness and relaxation.

(4) Assertiveness training—Cautela claims that assertiveness training is a crucial component to the treatment of clients who are generally anxious.

Cautela claimed to have treated 10 clients successfully with pervasive anxiety using this combination approach, but because he did not provide any objective outcome measures, this is difficult to evaluate.

Hutchings, Deaney, Basgall, and Houston (1980) assigned 70 students who scored high on self-report measures of general anxiety to one of five conditions: anxiety management training, consisting of PMRT; fantasy coping with anxiety-evoking situations and homework in real-life situations confronting situations giving rise to anxiety; two types of relaxation training; placebo treatment; or a no-treatment control group. Subjects assigned to anxiety management training had a significantly more favorable outcome than individuals in the other four groups. Relaxation training alone was found to be somewhat better than no treatment but inferior to the more structured anxiety management training. A 12-month follow-up, subjects assigned to anxiety management training remained more improved than the untreated clients. These results need to be tempered by the recognition that this study did not involve clients with GAD per se.

Barlow et al. (1984) treated five patients with GAD using EMG biofeedback-assisted relaxation training and cognitive behavior therapy and compared their outcomes with those of four GAD patients assigned to a waiting list control group. There were clear positive effects for most treated patients, as assessed by physiological measures, daily reports of background anxiety, and questionnaires. The control group remained virtually unchanged. The design of this study does not make it possible to partial out the relative impact of the two treatments (relaxation training versus cognitive restructuring), but the overall positive results are encouraging.

SUMMARY OF TREATMENT APPROACHES

It seems that the management of generalized anxiety disorder requires a great deal of flexibility on the part of the human service professional. The disorder is anomalous in that the symptomatic picture is often complex and difficult to diagnose and that no clear picture has emerged regarding the etiology of the condition. Promising approaches include supportive therapy with reassurance, short-term benzodiazepine therapy followed by a slow tapering off of drug use, and progressive muscular relaxation training, perhaps assisted by EMG biofeedback. Treatments based upon the principle of therapeutic exposure play a small role in the management of GAD unless specific anxiety-evoking cues can be isolated by the human service professional. The newer therapies based upon purported cognitive manipulations remain to be tested and have not been shown to be effective with a sample of patients with generalized anxiety.

It is fortunate that GAD is only rarely significantly disabling—most clients with this condition are usually able to continue to function without significant psychosocial limitations. The human service professional can expect to encounter comparatively few clients with this disorder. Most often clients who upon initial assessment appear to meet the criteria for generalized anxiety disorder are found upon more careful inquiry to be suffering from another primary anxiety disorder (e.g., panic disorder or pronounced social phobia) with secondary effects leading to complaints of pervasive anxiety.

FUTURE DIRECTIONS IN
GENERALIZED ANXIETY DISORDER

The DSM-III dropped the premise of its predecessors that anxiety neurosis was due to unconscious intrapsychic conflict leading to the development of maladaptive defense mechanisms. In fact, the whole concept of neurosis was eliminated as a diagnostic class. These were fairly radical changes, departing from a nosological consensus extending back over many decades. The human service professional struggling to assimilate the complexities of the DSM-III will no doubt be dismayed to learn that a task force is currently hard at work developing suggested revisions to the DSM-III, based upon emerging developments in research on the etiology and pathophysiology of mental disorders (Spitzer & Williams, 1985). Among the proposed revisions are the following:

(1) The current exclusion criteria for GAD specify that the symptoms must not be due to another mental disorder, such as depressive disorder or schizophrenia. The proposed revised exclusion criteria read, "Not due to a specific organic factor (e.g., hyperthyroidism, caffeine intoxication); has not occurred only during the course of an active phase of a psychotic disorder, or another anxiety disorder in which generalized anxiety is usually present, i.e., panic disorder, obsessive-compulsive disorder or post-traumatic stress disorder" (Spitzer & Williams, 1985, p. 766). The present chapter on GAD reflects these proposed changes.

(2) Spitzer and Williams (1985) propose (based upon clinical judgment only, not research findings) that the duration requirement for GAD be extended from one month to six months characterized by fairly continuous "nervousness or anxiety," "worry," or the "inability to relax." The rationale for this proposal is to help distinguish the individual with GAD from someone with a transient stress reaction.

(3) Currently, for an individual to be diagnosed as suffering from GAD the client must experience at least one symptom from three out of four areas (reviewed earlier in this chapter). It is proposed that the revised "criteria require the presence of at least six of an 18-item index of commonly associated symptoms taken from those currently listed in the DSM-III criteria" (Spitzer & Williams, 1985, p. 771).

Clearly, generalized anxiety disorder is a controversial diagnostic category. Some doubt that the disorder exists at all and others suggest that it is a precursor phase leading to the development of panic disorder (Sheehan & Sheehan, 1983). Akiskal (1985) strongly urges that clinical research on GAD be given a topic priority for the remainder of this century in an attempt to clarify the validity of the diagnosis and to develop effective therapies for the disorder. I concur.

REFERENCES

Abe, K., & Masui, T. (1981). Age-sex trends of phobic and anxiety symptoms in adolescents. *British Journal of Psychiatry, 138*, 297-302.

Ackerknect, E. H. (1968). *A short history of psychiatry* (2nd rev. ed., S. Wolff, trans.). New York: Hafner.

Agras, W. S., Chapin, H. H., & Oliveau, D. C. (1972). The natural history of phobia. *Archives of General Psychiatry, 26*, 315-317.

Agras, W. S., Sylvester, D., & Oliveau, D. C. (1969). The epidemiology of common fears and phobias. *Comprehensive Psychiatry, 10*, 151-156.

Akiskal, H. S. (1985). Anxiety: Definition, relationship to depression, and proposal for an integrative model. In A. H. Tuma & J. D. Maser (Eds.), *Anxiety and the anxiety disorders*. Hillsdale, NJ: Lawrence Erlbaum.

American Psychiatric Association. (1968). *Diagnostic and statistical manual of mental disorders* (2nd. ed.). Washington, DC: Author.

American Psychiatric Association. (1980). *Diagnostic and statistical manual of mental disorders* (3rd. ed.). Washington, DC: Author.

Arrindell, W. A. (1980). Dimensional structure and psychopathology correlates of the FSS(FSS-III) in a phobic population: A factorial definition of agoraphobia. *Behaviour Research and Therapy, 18*, 229-242.

Arrindell, W. A., & Emmelkamp, P. M. G. (1985). Psychological profile of the spouse of the female agoraphobic patient: Personality and symptomatology. *British Journal of Psychiatry, 146*, 405-414.

Ayllon, T., Smith, D., & Rogers, M. (1970). Behavioral management of school phobia. *Journal of Behavior Therapy and Experimental Psychiatry, 1*, 125-138.

Bailey, J. S., & Atchinson, T. (1969). The treatment of compulsive washing using reinforcement principles. *Behaviour Research and Therapy 7*, 327-329.

Bandura, A., & Rosenthal, T. L. (1966). Vicarious classical conditioning as a function of arousal level. *Journal of Personality and Social Psychology, 3*, 54-62.

Bandura, A., & Walters, R. H. (1963). *Social learning and personality development*. New York: Holt, Rinehart & Winston.

Barlow, D. H., Cohen, A. S., Waddel, M. T., Vermilyea, B. B., Klosko, J. S., Blanchard, E. B., & DiNardo, P. A. (1984). Panic and generalized anxiety disorders: Nature and treatment. *Behavior Therapy, 15*, 431-449.

Barlow, D. H., Leitenberg, H., Agras, W. S., & Wincze, J. P. (1969). The transfer gap in systematic desensitization: An analogue study. *Behaviour Research and Therapy, 7,* 191-196.

Barlow, D. H., & Wolfe, B. E. (1981). Behavioral approaches to anxiety disorders: A report on the NIHM-SUNY, Albany, research conference. *Journal of Consulting and Clinical Psychology, 49,* 448-454.

Bayer, R., & Spitzer, R. L. (1985). Neurosis, psychodynamics, and DSM-III: A history of the controversy. *Archives of General Psychiatry, 42,* 187-196.

Beck, A. T., & Emery, G. (1985). *Anxiety disorders and phobias: A cognitive perspective.* New York: Basic Books.

Benjamin, S., Marks, I. M., & Huson, J. (1972). Active muscular relaxation in desensitization of phobic patients. *Psychological Medicine, 2,* 381-390.

Berger, S. M. (1962). Conditioning through vicarious instigation. *Psychological Review, 69,* 450-466.

Bernstein, D. A., & Allen, G. J. (1969). Fear Survey Schedule (II): Normative data and factor analysis based upon a large college sample. *Behaviour Research and Therapy, 7,* 403-407.

Bernstein, D. A., & Borkovec, T. (1973). *Progressive relaxation training.* Champaign, IL: Research Press.

Bernstein, D. A., Kleinknecht, R. A., & Alexander, L. D. (1979). Antecedents of dental fear. *Journal of Public Health Dentistry, 39,* 113-124.

Blacker, K. H., & Levitt, M. (1979). The differential diagnosis of obsessive-compulsive symptoms. *Comprehensive Psychiatry, 20,* 532-547.

Bonn, J. A., Harrison, J., & Rees, L. (1973). Lactate infusion in the treatment of "free-floating" anxiety. *Canadian Psychiatric Association Journal, 18,* 41-46.

Bowen, R. C., & Kahout, J. (1979). The relationship between agoraphobia and primary affective disorders. *Canadian Journal of Psychiatry, 24,* 317-322.

Breier, A., Charney, D. S., & Heninger, G. R. (1984). Major depression in patients with agoraphobia and panic disorder. *Archives of General Psychiatry, 41,* 1129-1135.

Breuer, J., & Freud, S. (1966). *Studies in hysteria.* (Originally published in 1895.) New York: Avon.

Bridges, P. K., Goktepe, E. O., Maratos, J., Browne, A., & Young, L. (1973). A comparative review of patients with obsessional neurosis and with depression treated by psychosurgery. *British Journal of Psychiatry, 123,* 663-674.

Brown, I. (1974). Effects of perceived similarity on vicarious emotional conditioning. *Behaviour Research and Therapy, 12,* 165-173.

Calef, V. (1967). Alcoholism and ornithophobia in women. *Psychoanalytic Quarterly, 36,* 584-587.

Cameron, O. G. (1985). The differential diagnosis of anxiety. In G. C. Curtis, B. A. Thyer, & J. M. Rainey (Eds.), *The psychiatric clinics of North America: Anxiety disorders.* Philadelphia: W. B. Saunders.

Cameron, O. G., Curtis, G. C., Liepman, M., & Thyer, B. A. (in press) Ethanol intoxication impedes desensitization therapy for phobias. *British Journal of Psychiatry.*

Cameron, O. G., Thyer, B. A., Nesse, R. M., & Curtis, G. C. (1986) Symptom profiles of DSM-III anxiety disorders. *American Journal of Psychiatry, 143,* 1132-1137.

Campbell, W. G. (1982). Hypnosis for urinary retention. *American Journal of Psychiatry, 139,* 1082-1083.

Caplan, L. R. (1983). A logical approach to dizziness. *Drug Therapy* (August), pp. 40-43, 47-50, 55.

Cautela, J. R. (1966). A behavior therapy approach to pervasive anxiety. *Behaviour Research and Therapy, 4,* 99-109.

Chambless, D. L., Caputo, G. C., Bright, P., & Gallagher, R. (1984). Assessment of fear of fear in agoraphobics: The Body Sensations Questionnaire and the Agoraphobic Cognitions Questionnaire. *Journal of Consulting and Clinical Psychology, 52*, 1090-1097.

Chambless, D. L., Caputo, G. C., Jasin, S. E., Gracely, E. J., & Williams, C. (1985). The Mobility Inventory for Agoraphobia. *Behaviour Research and Therapy, 23*, 35-44.

Charney, D. S., Heninger, G. R. & Jatlow, P. I. (1985). Increased anxiogenic effects of caffeine in panic disorders. *Archives of General Psychiatry, 42*, 233-243.

Chouinard, G., Annable, L., Fontaine, R., & Solyom, L. (1982). Alprazolam in the treatment of generalized anxiety and panic disorders: A double-blind placebo-controlled study. *Psychopharmacology, 77*, 229-233.

Clark, D. A., & de Silva, P. (1985). The nature of anxious and intrusive thoughts: Distinct or uniform phenomena? *Behaviour Research and Therapy, 23*, 383-393.

Clark, D. F. (1963). The treatment of hysterical spasm and agoraphobia by behavior therapy. *Behaviour Research and Therapy, 1*, 245-250.

Clark, D. M., Salkovskis, P. A., & Chalkley, A. J. (1985). Respiratory control as a treatment for panic attacks. *Journal of Behavior Therapy and Experimental Psychiatry, 16*, 23-30.

Clouse, R. E., & Lustman, P. J. (1983). Psychiatric illness and contraction abnormalities of the esophagus. *New England Journal of Medicine, 309*, 1337-1342.

Cohen, S. D., Monteiro, W., & Marks, I. M. (1984). Two-year follow-up of agoraphobics after exposure and imipramine. *British Journal of Psychiatry, 144*, 276-281.

Connolly, J., Hallam, R., & Marks, I. M. (1976). Selective association of vaso-vagal fainting with blood-injury-illness fear. *Behavior Therapy, 1*, 8-13.

Cooke, D. J. (1979). Hyperventilation: Its treatment and relation to anxiety. *The Behavior Therapist, 2*(5), 32-33.

Cooper, J. E. (1963). A study of behavior therapy in 30 psychiatric patients. *Lancet, i*, 411-415.

Cooper, J. (1970). The Leyton Obsessional Inventory. *Psychological Medicine, 1*, 48-64.

Coryell, W., Noyes, R., & Clancy, J. (1982). Excess mortality in panic disorder: A comparison with primary unipolar depression. *Archives of General Psychiatry, 39*, 701-703.

Costello, C. G. (1970). Dissimilarities between conditioned avoidance responses and phobias. *Psychological Review, 7*, 250-254.

Craig, K. D., & Weinstein, M. S. (1965). Conditioning vicarious affective arousal. *Psychological Reports, 17*, 955-963.

Crowe, M., Marks, I. M., Agras, W. S., & Leitenberg, H. (1972). Time-limited desensitization, implosion and shaping for phobic patients: A crossover study. *Behaviour Research and Therapy, 10*, 319-328.

Crowe, R. R. (1985). Mitral valve prolapse and panic disorder. In G. C. Curtis, B. A. Thyer, & J. M. Rainey (Eds.), *The psychiatric clinics of North America: Anxiety disorders*. Philadelphia: W. B. Saunders.

Crowe, R. R., Noyes, R., Pauls, D., & Slymen, D. (1983). A family study of panic disorder. *Archives of General Psychiatry, 40*, 1065-1069.

Curlee, J., & Stern, H. (1973). The fear of heights among alcoholics. *Bulletin of the Menninger Clinic, 37*, 615-623.

Curtis, G. C. (1981). Sensory experiences during treatment of phobias by exposure *in vivo*. *American Journal of Psychiatry, 138*, 1095-1097.

Curtis, G. C., Cameron, O. G., & Nesse, R. M. (1982). The dexamethasone suppression test in panic disorder and agoraphobia. *American Journal of Psychiatiry, 139*, 1043-1046.

Curtis, G. C., Nesse, R. M., Buxton, M., Wright, J., & Lippman, D. (1976). Flooding *in vivo* as a research tool and treatment method for phobias: A preliminary report. *Comprehensive Psychiatry, 17,* 153-160.

Curtis, G. C., & Thyer, B. A. (1983). Fainting on exposure to phobic stimuli. *American Journal of Psychiatry, 140,* 771-774.

Davis, D., McLemore, C. W., & London, P. (1970). The role of visual imagery in desensitization. *Behaviour Research and Therapy, 8,* 11-13.

Derogatis, L., Lipman, R., & Covi, L. (1973). SCL-90: An outpatient rating scale—preliminary report. *Psychopharmacology Bulletin, 1,* 13-28.

Dietch, J. T. (1984). Cerebral tumor presenting with panic attacks. *Psychosomatics, 25,* 861-863.

Dimsdale, J., & Moss, J. (1980). Short-term catecholamine response to psychological stress. *Psychosomatic Medicine, 42,* 493-497.

DiNardo, P. A., O'Brien, G. T., Barlow, D. H., Waddell, M. T., & Blanchard, E. B. (1983). Reliability of DSM-III anxiety disorder categories using a new structured interview. *Archives of General Psychiatry, 40,* 1070-1074.

Dunn, C. (1983). Longitudinal records of anxiety and depression in general practice: The Second National Morbidity Study. *Psychological Medicine, 13,* 897-906.

Elie, R., & Lamontagne, Y. (1984). Alprazolam and diazepam in the treatment of generalized anxiety. *Journal of Clinical Psychopharmacology, 4,* 125-129.

Ellis, A. (Ed.). (1973). *Humanistic psychotherapy: The rational emotive approach.* New York: Julian Press.

Emery, J., & Krumboltz, J. (1967). Standard versus individualized hierarchies in desensitization to reduce test anxiety. *Journal of Counseling Psychology, 14,* 204-209.

Emmelkamp, P. M. G., & Wessells, H. (1975). Flooding in imagination versus flooding *in vivo:* A comparison with agoraphobics. *Behaviour Research and Therapy, 13,* 7-15.

Emmelkamp, P.M.G., Kuipers, A. C. & Eggeratt, J. B. (1978). Cognitive modification versus prolonged exposure in vivo: A comparison with agrophobics as subjects. *Behaviour Research and Therapy, 16,* 33-41.

Fazio, A. F. (1972). Implosive therapy with clinical phobias. *Journal of Abnormal Psychology, 80,* 183-188.

Ferenezi, S. (1926). The further development of an active therapy in psychoanalysis. In *Further Contributions to the Theory and Technigue of Psychoanalysis.* London: Hogarth Press.

Flament, M., & Rapoport, J. L. (1984). Childhood obsessive-compulsive disorder. In T. Insel (Ed.), *New findings in obsessive-compulsive disorder.* Washington, DC: American Psychiatric Press.

Foa, E. B. (1979). Failure in treating obsessive-compulsives. *Behaviour Research and Therapy, 17,* 169-176.

Foa, E. B., Grayson, J. B., & Steketee, G. S. (1982). Depression, habituation and treatment outcome in obsessive-compulsives. In J. Boulougouris (Ed.), *Learning theory approaches to psychiatry.* New York: John Wiley.

Foa, E. B., Grayson, J. B., Steketee, G. S., Doppelt, H. G., Turner, R. M., & Latimer, P. R. (1983). Success and failure in the behavior therapy of obsessive-compulsives. *Journal of Consulting and Clinical Psychology, 51,* 287-297.

Foa, E. B., Jameson, J. S., Turner, R. M., & Payne, L. L. (1980). Massed versus spaced exposure sessions in the treatment of agoraphobia. *Behaviour Research and Therapy, 18,* 333-338.

Foa, E. B., Steketee, G. S., & Groves, G. (1979). Use of behavioral therapy and imipramine: A case of obsessive-compulsive neurosis. *Behavior Modification, 3,* 419-430.

Foa, E. B., Steketee, G. S., Turner, R. M., & Fischer, S. C. (1980). Effects of imaginal exposure to feared disasters in obsessive-compulsive checkers. *Behaviour Research and Therapy, 18*, 449-455.

Freedman, A., Kaplan, H. I., & Sadock, B. J. (Eds.). (1976). *Modern synopsis of comprehensive handbook of psychiatry/II* (2nd ed.). Baltimore: Williams & and Wilkins.

Freud, S. (1955a). The justification for detaching from neurasthenia a particular syndrome: The anxiety neurosis. In J. Stachey (Ed.), *The standard edition of the complete psychological works of Sigmund Freud* (Vol. 1, pp. 78-106). London: Hogarth. (Originally published 1894.)

Freud, S. (1955b). A reply to criticisms on the anxiety neurosis. In J. Stachey (Ed.), *The standard edition of the complete psychological works of Sigmund Freud* (Vol. 1). London: Hogarth. (Originally published 1895.)

Freud, S. (1955c). Notes upon a case of obsessional neurosis. In J. Stachey (Ed.), *The standard edition of the complete psychological works of Sigmund Freud* (Vol. 10, pp. 153-318). London: Hogarth. (Originally published 1909.)

Freud, S. (1955d). Lines of advance in psychoanalytic theory. In J. Strachey (Ed.), *The standard edition of the complete psychological works of Sigmund Freud* (Vol. 17, pp. 159-168). London: Hogarth. (Originally published 1918.)

Freud, S. (1959). *Inhibitions, symptoms and anxiety.* New York: Norton. (Originally published 1926.)

Freud, S. (1962). Obsessions and compulsions. In J. Strachey (Ed.), *The standard edition of the complete psychological works of Sigmund Freud* (Vol. 3, pp. 81). London: Hogarth.

Freud, S. (1963). *The standard edition of the complete psychological works of Sigmund Freud* (Vol. 16, pp. 392-411). London: Hogarth Press.

Fyer, A., Leibowitz, M. R., Gorman, J., Davies, S. O., & Klein, D. F. (1983). Sodium lactate reinfusion of recovered lactate-vulnerable panic disorder patients. *Psychopharmacology Bulletin, 19,* 576-577.

Gabe, J., & Lipshitz-Phillips, S. (1984). Tranquilizers as social control? *The Sociological Review, 32,* 524-546.

Gardos, G. (1981). Is agoraphobia a psychosomatic form of depression? In D. F. Klein & J. G. Rabkin (Eds.), *Anxiety: New research and changing concepts.* New York: Raven.

Geer, J. H. (1965). The development of a scale to measure fear. *Behaviour Research and Therapy, 3,* 45-53.

Gerz, H. O. (1962). The treatment of the phobic and the obsessive-compulsive patient using paradoxical instruction. *Journal of Neuropsychiatry, 3,* 375-387.

Ghosh, A., Marks, I. M., & Carr, A. C. (1984). Controlled study of self-exposure treatment: A preliminary communication. *Journal of the Royal Society of Medicine, 77,* 483-487.

Gorman, J. M., Levy, G. F., Liebowitz, M. R., McGrath, P., Appleby, I. L., Dillon, D. J., Davies, S. O., & Klein, D. F. (1984). Effect of acute beta-adrenergic blockade on lactate-induced panic. *Archives of General Psychiatry, 40,* 1079-1082.

Gorman, J. M., Martinez, J. M., Liebowitz, M. R., Fyer, A. J., & Klein, D. F. (1984). Hypoglycemia and panic attacks. *American Journal of Psychiatry 141,* 101-102.

Gonzalez, E. R. (1982). Panic disorder may respond to new "antidepressants." *Journal of the American Medical Association, 248,* 3077-3087.

Gray, M. (1978). *Neuroses: A comprehensive and critical view.* New York: Van Nostrand Rinehold.

Greist, J. H., Marks, I. M., Berlin, F., Gourney, K., & Noshivani, H. (1980). Avoidance versus confrontation of fear. *Behavior Therapy, 11*, 1-14.

Griez, E., & van den Hout, M. A. (1983). Treatment of phobophobia by exposure to carbon-dioxide-induced anxiety symptoms. *Journal of Nervous and Mental Disease, 177*, 506-508.

Grinker, R. R., MacGregor, H., Selan, K., Klein, A., & Kohrman, J. (1961). *Psychiatric social work: A transactional case book.* New York: Basic Books.

Guttmacher, L. B., & Nelles, C. (1984). *In vivo* desensitization alteration of lactate-induced panic: A case study. *Behavior Therapy, 15*, 369-372.

Hagman, E. (1932). A study of fears of pre-school age. *Journal of Experimental Education, 1*, 110-130.

Hall, G. S. (1987). A study of fears. *American Journal of Psychology, 8*, 147-249.

Hallam, R. S. (1974). Extinction of ruminations: A case study. *Behavior Therapy, 5*, 565-568.

Hand, I., Lamontagne, Y., & Marks, I. M. (1974). Group exposure (flooding) *in vivo* for agoraphobics. *British Journal of Psychiatry, 124*, 588-602.

Harris, E., Noyes, R., Pauls, D. et al. (1983). A family study of panic disorder. *Archives of General Psychiatry, 40*, 1061-1064.

Heide, F. J., & Borkovec, T. D. (1984). Relaxation-induced anxiety: Mechanisms and theoretical implications. *Behaviour Research and Therapy, 22*, 1-12.

Herrnstein, R. (1969). Method and theory in the study of avoidance. *Psychological Review, 76*, 49-69.

Hersen, M. (1970). Behavior modification approach to a school phobia case. *Journal of Clinical Psychology, 26*, 128-132.

Hersen, M. (1971). The behavioral treatment of school phobia. *Journal of Nervous and Mental Disease, 153*, 99-107.

Hersen, M. (1973). Self-assessment of fear. *Behavior Therapy, 4*, 241-257.

Herzberg, A. (1941). Short treatment of neuroses by graduated tasks. *British Journal of Medical Psychology,19*, 22-36.

Himle, D. P., & Shorkey, C. (1973). The systematic desensitization of a car phobia and the recall of a related memory. *Journal of Biological Psychology,* 15(1), 4-7.

Himle, D. P., Thyer, B. A., & Papsdorf, J. D. (1982). Relationships between irrational beliefs and anxiety. *Cognitive Therapy and Research, 6*, 219-223.

Himle, D. P., Thyer, B. A., Papsdorf, J. D., & Caldwell, S. (1984). *In vivo* distraction-coping training in the treatment of test anxiety: A one-year follow-up study. *Journal of Clinical Psychology,40*, 458-462.

Hodgson, R. J., & Rachman, S. J. (1977). Obsessive-compulsive complaints. *Behaviour Research and Therapy, 15*, 389-395.

Hoehn-Saric, R., & McLeod, D. R. (1985). Generalized anxiety disorder. In G. C. Curtis, B. A. Thyer, & J. M. Rainey (Eds.), *The psychiatric clinics of North America: Anxiety disorders.* Philadelphia: W. B. Saunders.

Hoelscher, T. J., Lichstein, K. L., & Rosenthal, T. L. (1984). Objective versus subjective assessment of relaxation compliance among anxious individuals. *Behaviour Research and Therapy, 22*, 187-193.

Holmes, D. S. (1984). Meditation and somatic arousal reduction: A review of the experimental evidence. *American Psychologist, 39*, 1-10.

Hudson, W. R. (1982). *The clinical measurement package: A field manual.* Chicago: Dorsey Press.

Hudson, W. R., & Thyer, B. A. (1986). Research measures and indices in direct practice. In A. Minahan (Ed.), *Encyclopedia of social work.* Washington, DC: National Association of Social Workers.

Hugdahl, K. (1978). Electrodermal conditioning to potentially phobic stimuli: Effects of instructed extinction. *Behaviour Research and Therapy, 16,* 315-321.

Hutchings, D. F., Deaney, D. R., Basgall, J., & Houston, B. K. (1980). Anxiety management and applied relaxation in reducing general anxiety. *Behaviour Research and Therapy, 18,* 181-190.

Hygge, S., & Ohman, A. (1978). Modeling processes in the acquisition of fears: Vicarious electrodermal conditioning to fear-relevent stimuli. *Journal of Personality and Social Psychology, 36,* 271-279.

Huxley, A. (1962). *Island.* New York: Bantam.

Ilg, F. L., & Ames, L. B. (1955). *Child behavior.* New York: Dell.

Insel, T. R., & Murphy, D. L. (1981). The psychopharmacological treatment of obsessive-compulsive disorder: A review. *Journal of Clinical Psychopharmacology, 1,* 304-311.

Jablensky, A. (1985). Approaches to the definition and classification of anxiety and anxiety related disorders in European psychiatry. In A. H. Tuma & J. D. Maser (Eds.), *Anxiety and the anxiety disorders.* Hillsdale, NJ: Lawrence Erlbaum.

Jannoun, L., Munby, M., Catalan, J., & Gelder, M. (1980). A home-based treatment program for agoraphobia: Replication and controlled evaluation. *Behavior Therapy, 11,* 294-305.

Jansson, L., & Ost, L. (1982). Behavioral treatments for agoraphobia: An evaluative review. *Clinical Psychology Review, 2,* 311-336.

Jenike, M. A. (1983). Obsessive-compulsive disorder. *Comprehensive Psychiatry, 24,* 99-115.

Jersild, A. T. (1968). *Child psychology* (6th ed.). Englewood Cliffs, NJ: Prentice-Hall.

John, E. (1941). A study of the effects of evacuation and air raids on preschool children. *British Journal of Educational Psychology, 11,* 173-182.

Johnston, D., & Gath, D. (1973). Arousal levels and attribution effects in diazepam-assisted flooding. *British Journal of Psychiatry, 122,* 463-466.

Johnston, D. W., Lancashire, M., Mathews, A. M., Munby, M., Shaw, P. M., & Gelder, M. G. (1976). Imaginal flooding and exposure to real phobic situations: Changes during treatment. *British Journal of Psychiatry, 129,* 272-277.

Jones, B. A. (1984). Panic attacks with panic masked by alexithymia. *Psychosomatics, 25,* 858-859.

Kandel, E. R. (1983). From metapsychology to molecular biology: Explorations into the nature of anxiety. *American Journal of Psychiatry, 140,* 1277-1293.

Kellerman, J. (1981). *Helping the fearful child.* New York: Norton.

Kerber, K., Cameron, O. G., Curtis, G. C., & Thyer, B. A. (1986). *Obsessive-compulsive disorder and the dexamethasone suppression test: A replication.* Manuscript submitted for publication.

Kirk, J. (1983). Behavioral treatment of obsessive-compulsive patients in routine clinical practice. *Behaviour Research and Therapy, 21,* 57-62.

Klein, D. F. (1964). Delineation of two drug-responsive anxiety syndromes. *Psychopharmacologia, 5,* 397-408.

Klein, D. F. (1981). Anxiety reconceptualized. In D. F. Klein & J. G. Rabkin (Eds.), *Anxiety: New research and changing concepts.* New York: Raven.

Klein, D. F., & Fink, M. (1962). Psychiatric reaction patterns to imipramine. *American Journal of Psychiatry, 119,* 432-438.

Klein, D. F., Gittelman, R., Quitkin, F., & Rifkin, A. (1980). *Diagnosis and drug treatment of psychiatric disorders.* Baltimore: Williams & Wilkins.

Kleinknecht, R. A., Klepac, R. K., & Alexander, L. D. (1973). Origins and characteristics of fears of dentistry. *Journal of the American Dental Association, 86,* 842-848.

Kraft, T. (1971). Social anxiety model of alcoholism. *Perceptual and Motor Skills, 33,* 797-798.

Kringlen, E. (1965). Obsessional neurotics: A long-term follow-up. *British Journal of Psychiatry, 111,* 709-722.

Kwentus, J. A., Achilles, J. T., & Goyer, P. F. (1982). Hypoglycemia: Etiologic and psychosomatic aspects of diagnosis. *Postgraduate Medicine, 71,* 99-104.

Lamontagne, Y., & Marks, I. M. (1973). Psychogenic urinary retention: Treatment by prolonged exposure. *Behavior Therapy, 4,* 581-585.

Lang, P. J., & Lazovick, A. D. (1963). The experimental desensitization of a phobia. *Journal of Abnormal and Social Psychology, 66,* 519-525.

Lang, P. J., Lazovick, A. D., & Reynolds, D. J. (1965). Desensitization, suggestability and pseudotherapy. *Journal of Abnormal Psychology, 70,* 395-402.

Lapouse, R., & Monk, M. A. (1959). Fears and worries in a representative sample of children. *American Journal of Orthopsychiatry, 29,* 803-818.

Lazarus, A. A. (1971). *Behavior therapy and beyond.* New York: McGraw-Hill.

Lazarus, A. A., Davison, G., & Polefka, D. (1965). Classical and operant factors in the treatment of school phobia. *Journal of Abnormal Psychology, 70,* 225-229.

Leckman, J. F., Weissman, M. M., Merikangas, K. R., Pauls, D. L., & Prusoff, B. A. (1983). Panic disorder and major depression. *Archives of General Psychiatry, 40,* 1055-1060.

Leibowitz, M. R. (1985). Imipramine in the treatment of panic disorder and its complications. In G. C. Curtis, B. A. Thyer, & J. M. Rainey (Eds.), *The psychiatric clinics of North America: Anxiety disorders.* Philadelphia: W. B. Saunders.

Levy, A. B. (1984). Delirium and seizures due to abrupt alprazolam withdrawal: Case report. *Journal of Clinical Psychiatry, 45,* 38-39.

Lewis, A. (1976). A note of classifying phobia. *Psychological Medicine, 6,* 21-22.

Ley, R. (1985). Agoraphobia, the panic attack and the hyperventilation syndrome. *Behaviour Research and Therapy, 23,* 79-81.

Lieberman, J. A., Brenner, R., Lesser, M., Cocarro, E., Borenstein, M., & Kane, J. M. (1983). Dexamethasone suppression test in patients with panic disorder. *American Journal of Psychiatry, 140,* 917-919.

Likierman, H., & Rachman, S. (1982). Obsessions: An experimental investigation of thought stopping and habituation training. *Behavioural Psychotherapy, 10,* 324-338.

Lindemann, C. G., Zitrin, C. M., & Klein, D. F. (1984). Thyroid dysfunction in phobic patients. *Psychosomatics, 25,* 603-606.

Linden, W. (1981). Exposure treatments for focal phobias. *American Journal of Psychiatry, 38,* 769-775.

Lum, L. (1977). Breathing exercises in the treatment of hyperventilation and chronic anxiety states. *Chest, Heart and Stroke Journal, 2,* 6-11.

Malleson, N. (1959). Panic and phobia: Possible method of treatment. *Lancet, 1,* 225-227.

Manchanda, R., Sethi, B., & Gupta, S. (1979). Hostility and guilt in obsessive-compulsive neurosis. *British Journal of Psychiatry, 135,* 52-54.

Manesevitz, M., & Lanyon, R. I. (1965). Fear Survey Schedule: A normative study. *Psychological Reports, 17,* 699-703.

Marks, I. M. (1969). *Fears and phobias.* New York: Academic Press.

Marks, I. M. (1978). *Living with fear.* New York: McGraw-Hill.

Marks, I. M. (1981). *Cure and care of the neuroses.* New York: John Wiley.

Marks, I. M. (1982). Is conditioning relevent to behavior therapy? In J. C. Boulougouris (Ed.), *Learning theory approaches to psychiatry.* New York: John Wiley.

Marks, I. M. (1983a). Are there antiphobic or antipanic drugs? Review of the evidence. *British Journal of Psychiatry, 143,* 338-347.

Marks, I. M. (1983b). Panic attacks in phobia treatment—In reply. *Archives of General Psychiatry, 40,* 1151.

Marks, I. M. (1985). Behavioral psychotherapy for anxiety disorders. In. G. C. Curtis, B. A. Thyer, & J. M. Rainey (Eds.), *The psychiatric clinics of North America: Anxiety disorders.* Philadelphia: W. B. Saunders.

Marks, I. M., & Gelder, M. G. (1965). A controlled retrospective study of behaviour therapy in phobic patients. *British Journal of Psychiatry, 111,* 561-573.

Marks, I. M., Gray, S., Cohen, D., Hill, R., Mawson, D., Ramm, E., & Stern, R. (1983). Imipramine and brief therapist-aided exposure in agoraphobics having self-exposure homework. *Archives of General Psychiatry, 40,* 153-162.

Marks, I. M., & Mathews, A. M. (1979). Brief standard self-ratings for phobic patients. *Behaviour Research and Therapy, 17,* 263-267.

Marks, I. M., Stern, R. S., Mawson, D., Cobb, J., & McDonald, R. (1980). Clomipramine and exposure of obsessive-compulsive rituals. I. *British Journal of Psychiatry, 136,* 1-25.

Masserman, J. H. (1943). *Behavior and neuroses.* Chicago: University of Chicago Press.

Masserman, J. H., Jacques, M. G., & Nicholson, M. R. (1945). Alcohol as a preventive of experimental neuroses. *Psychosomatic Medicine, 6,* 281-299.

Masserman, J. H., & Yum, K. S. (1946). An analysis of the influence of alcohol on experimental neuroses in cats. *Psychosomatic Medicine, 8,* 36-52.

Mathews, A. (1978). Fear reduction research and clinical phobias. *Psychological Bulletin, 85,* 390-404.

Mathews, A. M., Gelder, M. G., & Johnston, D. W. (1981). *Agoraphobia: Nature and treatment.* New York: Guilford.

Mathews, A. M., Johnston, D. W., Shaw, P. M., & Gelder, M. G. (1974). Process variables and the prediction of outcome in behavior therapy. *British Journal of Psychiatry, 123,* 445-462.

Matson, J. L. (1981). A controlled outcome study of phobias in mentally retarded adults. *Behaviour Research and Therapy, 19,* 101-107.

Mavissakalian, M., & Michelson, L. (1983a). Tricyclic antidepressants in obsessive-compulsive disorder: Antiobsessional or antidepressant agents? *Journal of Nervous and Mental Disease, 171,* 301-306.

Mavissakalian, M., & Michelson, L. (1983b). Agoraphobia: Behavioral and pharama-cological treatment. *Psychopharmacology Bulletin, 19,* 116-118.

Mavissakalian, M., Turner, S. M., Michelson, L., & Jacob, R. (1985). Tricylic antidepressants in obsessive-compulsive disorder: Antiobsessional or antipressant agents? II. *American Journal of Psychiatry, 142,* 572-576.

McCormick, S. R., Nielsen, J., & Jatlow, P. I. (1985). Alprazolam overdose: Clinical findings and serum concentrations in two cases. *Journal of Clinical Psychiatry, 46,* 247-248.

McDonald, G. W., Fisher, G. F., & Burnham, C. (1965). Reproducibility of the oral glucose tolerance test. *Diabetes, 14,* 473-480.

McIntyre, J. S., & Romano, J. (1977). Is there a stethoscope in the house (and is it used?). *Archives of General Psychiatry, 34,* 1147-1151.

McKeon, J., Roa, B., & Mann, A. (1984). Life events and personality traits in obsessive-compulsive neurosis. *British Journal of Psychiatry, 144,* 185-189.

McNair, D. M., & Kahn, R. J. (1981). Imipramine compared with a benzodiazepine for agoraphobia. In D. F. Klein & J. Rabkin (Eds.), *Anxiety: New research and changing concepts.* New York: Raven Press.

McNally, R. J. (1981). Phobias and preparedness: Instructional reversal of electrodermal conditioning to fear-relevent stimuli. *Psychological Reports, 48,* 175-180.

Melville, J. (1977). *Phobias and obsessions.* New York: Penguin.

Mendel, J.G.C., & Klein, D. F. (1969). Anxiety attacks with subsequent agoraphobia. *Comprehensive Psychiatry, 10,* 190-195.

Meyer, V. (1957). The treatment of two phobic patients on the basis of learning principles. *Journal of Abnormal and Social Psychology, 55,* 261-266.

Michelson, L., & Mavissakalian, M. (1985). Psychophysiological outcome of behavioral and pharmacological treatments for agoraphobia. *Journal of Consulting and Clinical Psychology, 53,* 229-236.

Miles, H. H. W., Barabee, E. L., & Finesinger, J. E. (1961). Evaluation of psychotherapy with follow-up study of 62 cases of anxiety neurosis. *Psychosomatic Medicine, 13,* 83-103.

Mitchell-Heggs, N., Kelly, D., & Richardson, A. (1976). Sterotactic limbic leucotomy: A follow-up at 16 months. *British Journal of Psychiatry, 128,* 226-240.

Mittan, R. J. (1983). *Patients' fears about seizures: A greater psychosocial stressor?* Paper presented at the International Epilepsy Symposium, Washington, DC.

Morris, R. J., & Kratochwill, T. R. (1983). *Treating children's fears and phobias: A behavioral approach.* New York: Pergamon.

Moss, A., & Wynar, B. (1970). Tachycardia in house officers presenting cases at grand rounds. *Annals of Internal Medicine, 72,* 255-256.

Mowrer, O. H. (1939). A stimulus-response theory of anxiety and its role as a reinforcing agent. *Psychological Review, 46,* 553-565.

Mullaney, J., & Trippett, C. (1979). Alcohol dependence and phobias: Clinical description and relevence. *British Journal of Psychiatry, 135,* 565-573.

Myers, J. K., Weissman, M. M., Tischler, G. L., Holzer, C. E., Leaf, P. J., Orvaschel, H., Anthony, J. C., Boyd, J. N., Burke, J. D., Kramer, M., & Stoltzman, R. (1984). Six-month prevalence of psychiatric disorders in three communities. *Archives of General Psychiatry, 41,* 959-967.

National Academy of Sciences (1979). *Sleeping pills, insomnia and medical practice: Report of a study of the Institute of Medicine.* Washington, DC: Author.

Nesse, R. M., Curtis, G. C., Thyer, B. A., McCann, D., Huber-Smith, M., & Knopf, R. F. (1985). Endocrine and cardiovascular responses during phobic anxiety. *Psychosomatic Medicine, 47,* 320-332.

Norton, G. R., Allen, G. E., & Hilton, J. (1983). The social validity of treatments for agoraphobia. *Behaviour Research and Therapy, 21,* 393-399.

Noyes, R. (1982). Beta-blocking drugs and anxiety. *Psychosomatics, 23,* 155-170.

Noyes, R. (1985). Beta-adrenergic blocking drugs in anxiety and stress. In G. C. Curtis, B. A. Thyer, & J. M. Rainey (Eds.), *The psychiatric clinics of North America: Anxiety disorders.* Philadelphia: W. B. Saunders.

Noyes, R., Clancy, J., Crowe, R., Hoenk, P. R., & Slymen, D. J. (1978). The familial prevalence of anxiety neurosis. *Archives of General Psychiatry, 35,* 1057-1059.

Ohman, A., Eriksson, A., & Olofsson, C. (1975). One-trial learning and superior resistance to extinction of autonomic responses conditioned to potentially phobic stimuli. *Journal of Comparative and Physiological Psychology, 88,* 699-627.

Ollendick, T. H. (1983). Reliability and validity of the revised Fear Survey Schedule for children (FSSC-R). *Behaviour Research and Therapy, 21,* 685-692.

Ollendick, T. H., & Nettle, M. D. (1977). An evaluation of the relaxation component of induced anxiety. *Behavior Therapy, 8,* 561-566.

Omer, H. (1985). Fulfillment of therapeutic tasks as a precondition for acceptance in therapy. *American Journal of Psychotherapy, 39,* 175-186.

Orwin, A. (1973). "The running treatment": A preliminary communication on a new use for an old therapy (physical activity) in the agoraphobic syndrome. *British Journal of Psychiatry, 122,* 175-179.

Ost, L., & Hugdahl, H. (1981). Acquisition of phobias and anxiety response patterns in clinical patients. *Behaviour Research and Therapy, 19*, 439-447.

Ost, L. & Hugdahl, K. (1985). Acquisition of blood and dental phobia and anxiety response patterns in clinical patients. *Behaviour and Research Therapy, 23,* 27-34.

Papsdorf, J. D., Himle, D. P., McCann, B. S., & Thyer, B. A. (1982). Anagram solution time and the effects of distraction, sex differences, and anxiety. *Perceptual and Motor Skills, 55,* 215-222.

Parker, G. (1979). Reported parental characteristics of agoraphobics and social phobics. *British Journal of Psychiatry, 135,* 555-560.

Parkinson, L., & Rachman, S. (1980). Are intrusive thoughts subject to habituation? *Behaviour Research and Therapy, 18,* 409-418.

Paul, G. L. (1966). *Insight versus desensitization in psychotherapy: An experiment in anxiety reduction.* Palo Alto, CA: Stanford University Press.

Paul, G. L. (1969). Outcome of systematic desensitization II: Controlled investigations of individual treatment, technique variations and current status. In C. M. Franks (Ed.), *Behavior therapy: Appraisal and status.* New York: McGraw-Hill.

Pinto, R. (1972). A case of movement epilepsy with agoraphobia treated by flooding. *British Journal of Psychiatry, 121,* 287-288.

Pollitt, J., & Young, J. (1971). Anxiety state or masked depression: A study based on the action of monoamine oxidase inhibitors. *British Journal of Psychiatry, 119,* 143-149.

Quitkin, F., Rifkin, A., Kaplan, J., & Klein, D. F. (1972). Phobic anxiety syndrome complicated by drug dependence and addiction, a treatable form of drug abuse. *Archives of General Psychiatry, 27,* 159-162.

Rachman, S. (1968). The role of muscular relaxation in desensitization therapy. *Behaviour Research and Therapy, 6,* 159-166.

Rachman, S. (1974). Primary obsessional slowness. *Behaviour Research and Therapy, 11,* 463-471.

Rachman, S. (1976). The passing of the two-stage theory of fear and avoidance: Fresh possibilities *Behaviour Research and Therapy 14,* 125-131.

Rachman, S., & de Silva, P. (1978). Abnormal and normal obsessions. *Behaviour Research and Therapy, 16,* 233-248.

Rachman, S., & Hodgson, R. J. (1980). *Obsessions and compulsions.* Englewood Cliffs, NJ: Prentice-Hall.

Rainey, J. M., Ettedgui, E., Pohl, R. B., & Bridges, M. (1985). Effects of acute beta-adrenergic blockade on lactate-induced panic (letter). *Archives of General Psychiatry, 42,* 104-105.

Rainey, J. M., & Nesse, R. M. (1985). Psychobiology of anxiety and anxiety disorders. In G. C. Curtis, B. A. Thyer, & J. M. Rainey (Eds.), *The psychiatric clinics of North America: Anxiety disorders.* Philadelphia: W. B. Saunders.

Rainey, J. M., Pohl, R. B., Williams, M., Knitter, E., Freedman, R. R., & Ettegui, E. (1984). A comparison of lactate and isoproterenol anxiety states. *Psychopathology, 17,* 74-82.

Ramm, E., Marks, I. M., Yuksel, S., & Stern, R. S. (1981). Anxiety management training for anxiety states: Positive compared to negative self-statements. *British Journal of Psychiatry, 140,* 367-373.

Rapee, R. M. (1985). A case of panic disorder treated with breathing retraining. *Journal of Behavior Therapy and Experimental Psychiatry, 16,* 63-65.

Raulin, M. L., & Wee, J. L. (1984). The development and initial validation of a scale to measure social fear. *Journal of Clinical Psychology, 40,* 780-784.

Rickels, K. (1983). Nonbenzodiazepine anxiolytics: Clinical usefulness. *Journal of Clinical Psychiatry, 44,* 38-43.

Rickels, K., Case, G., Downing, R. W., & Winokur, A. (1983). Long-term diazepam therapy and clinical outcome. *Journal of the American Medical Association*, 250, 767-771.

Rickels, K., Weissman, K., Norstad, N., Singer, M., Stoltz, D., Brown, A., & Danton, J. (1982). Buspirone and diazepam in anxiety: A controlled study. *Journal of Clinical Psychiatry*, 43, 81-86.

Rifkin, A. (1983). Panic disorder: Response to sodium lactate, and treatment with antidepressants. *Psychopharmacology Bulletin*, 19, 432-434.

Rimm, D., Briddle, D., Zimmerman, M., & Caddy, G. (1981). The effects of alcohol and the expectancy of alcohol on snake fear. *Addictive Behaviors*, 6, 47-51.

Rimm, D., Janda, L. H., Lancaster, D. W., Nahl, M., & Dittmar, K. (1977). An exploratory investigation of the origin and maintenance of phobias. *Behaviour Research and Therapy*, 15, 231-238.

Roberts, A. H. (1964). Housebound housewives: A follow-up study of a phobic anxiety state. *British Journal of Psychiatry*, 110, 191-197.

Roberts, A. H. (1985). Biofeedback: Research, training and clinical roles. *American Psychologist*, 40, 938-941.

Robins, L. N., Helzer, J. E., Weissman, M. M., Orvaschel, H., Gruenberg, E., Burke, J. D., & Regier, D. A. (1984). Lifetime prevalence of specific psychiatric disorders in three sites. *Archives of General Psychiatry*, 41, 949-958.

Rosenbaum, J. F., Woods, S. W., Groves, J. E., & Klerman, G. L. (1984). Emergence of hostility during alprazolam treatment. *American Journal of Psychiatry*, 141, 792-793.

Salkovskis, P. M. (1983). Treatment of an obsessional patient using habituation to audiotaped ruminations. *British Journal of Clinical Psychology*, 22, 311-313.

Salkovskis, P. M., & Harrison, J. (1984). Abnormal and normal obsessions: A replication. *Behaviour Research and Therapy*, 22, 549-552.

Salzman, L. (1966). Therapy of obsessional states. *American Journal of Psychiatry, 122*, 1139-1146.

Salzman, L., & Thaler, F. H. (1981). Obsessive-compulsive disorders: A review of the literature. *American Journal of Psychiatry*, 138, 286-296.

Sandler, J., & Hazari, A. (1960). The "obsessional": On the psychological classification of obsessional character traits and symptoms. *British Journal of Medical Psychology, 33*, 113-122.

Schacht, T., & Nathan, P. (1977). But is it good for psychologists? Appraisal and status of DSM-III. *American Psychologist*, 32, 1017-1025.

Scherer, M. W., & Nakamura, C. Y. (1968). A fear survey schedule for children (FSS-FC): A factor-analytic comparison with manifest anxiety. *Behaviour Research and Therapy*, 6, 173-182.

Seligman, M. E. (1971). Phobias and preparedness. *Behavior Therapy*, 2, 307-320.

Sheehan, D. V. (1982). Panic attacks and phobias. *New England Journal of Medicine, 307*, 156-158.

Sheehan, D. V. (1985). Monoamine oxidase inhibitors and alprazolam in the treatment of panic disorder and agoraphobia. In G. C. Curtis, B. A. Thyer, & J. M. Rainey (Eds.), *The psychiatric clinics of North America: Anxiety disorders*. Philadelphia: W. B. Saunders.

Sheehan, D. V., Ballenger, J., & Jacobson, G. (1980). Treatment of endogenous anxiety with phobic, hysterical and hypochondriacal symptoms. *Archives of General Psychiatry*, 37, 51-59.

Sheehan, D. V., Carr, D. B., Fishman, S. M., Walsh, M. M., & Peltier-Saxe, D. (1985). Lactate infusion in anxiety research: Its evolution and practice. *Journal of Clinical Psychiatry*, 46, 158-165.

Sheehan, D. V., & Sheehan, K. H. (1982a). The classification of anxiety and hysterical states. Part I. Historical review and empirical delineation. *Journal of Clinical Psychopharmacology, 2,* 235-243.

Sheehan, D. V., & Sheehan, K. H. (1982b). The classification of anxiety and hysterical states. Part II. Toward a more heuristic classification. *Journal of Clinical Psychopharmacology, 2,* 386-393.

Sheehan, D. V., & Sheehan, K. H. (1983). The classification of phobic disorders. *International Journal of Psychiatry in Medicine, 12,* 243-266.

Shelton, J. L., & Levy, R. L. (1981). *Behavioral assignments and treatment compliance.* Champaign, IL: Research Press.

Sherman, A. R. (1972). Real-life exposure as a primary therapeutic factor in desensitization treatment of fear. *Journal of Abnormal Psychology, 79,* 19-28.

Shorkey, C., & Himle, D. P. (1974). Systematic desensitization treatment of a recurring nightmare and related insomnia. *Journal of Behavior Therapy and Experimental Psychiatry, 5,* 97-98.

Silverman, P. J. (1977). The role of social reinforcement in maintaining obsessive-compulsive neurosis. *Behaviour Research and Therapy, 8,* 325-326.

Sinnott, A., Jones, R. B., Scott-Fordham, A., & Woodward, R. (1981). Augmentation of *in vivo* exposure treatment for agoraphobia by the formulation of neighborhood self-help groups. *Behaviour Research and Therapy, 19,* 339-347.

Smail, P., Stockwell, T., Canter, S., & Hodgson, R. (1984). Alcohol dependence and phobic anxiety states I: A prevalence study. *British Journal of Psychiatry, 144,* 53-57.

Smith, M. J. (1977). *Kicking the fear habit.* New York: Bantam.

Solomon, K., & Hart, R. (1978). Pitfalls and prospects in clinical research on antianxiety drugs: benzodiazepine and placebo—A research review. *Journal of Clinical Psychiatry, 39,* 61-69.

Spielberger, C. D., Gorsuch, R., & Lushene, R. (1970). *Manual for the State-Trait Anxiety Inventory.* Palo Alto, CA: Consulting Psychologists' Press.

Spitzer, R. L., & Williams, J. B. W. (1983). The revision of DSM-III. *Psychiatric Annals, 13,* 808-811.

Spitzer, R. L., & Williams, J. B. W. (1985). Proposed revisions in the DSM-III classification of anxiety disorders based on research and clinical experience. In A. H. Tuma & J. D. Maser (Eds.), *Anxiety and anxiety disorders.* Hillsdale, NJ: Lawrence Erlbaum.

Stambaugh, E. E. (1977). Audiotaped flooding in outpatient treatment of somatic complaints. *Journal of Behavior Therapy and Experimental Psychiatry, 8,* 173-176.

Stern, R., & Marks, I. M. (1973). Brief and prolonged flooding. *Archives of General Psychiatry, 28,* 270-276.

Stockwell, T., Smail, P., Hodgson, R., & Canter, S. (1984). Alcohol dependence and phobic anxiety states II: A retrospective study. *British Journal of Psychiatry, 144,* 58-63.

Strahan, A., Rosenthal, J., Kaswan, M., & Winston, A. (1985). Three case reports of acute paroxysmal excitement associated with alprazolam treatment. *American Journal of Psychiatry, 142,* 859-861.

Sue, D. (1972). The role of relaxation in systematic desensitization. *Behaviour Research and Therapy, 10,* 153-158.

Tallman, J. F., Paul, S. M., Skolnick, P., & Gallagher, D. W. (1980). Receptors for the age of anxiety: Pharmacology of the benzodiazepines. *Science, 207,* 274-281.

Task Force on Nomenclature and Statistics, American Psychiatric Association. (1977). *Diagnostic and statistical manual* (3rd ed., draft version of April 15, 1977). Washington, DC: American Psychiatric Association.

Teasdale, J. D., Walsh, P. A., Lancashire, M., & Mathews, A. M. (1977). Group exposure for agoraphobics: A replication study. *British Journal of Psychiatry, 130,* 186-193.

Telch, M. T., Agras, W. S., Taylor, C. B., Roth, W. T., & Gallen, C. C. (1985). Combined pharmacological and behavioral treatment for agoraphobia. *Behaviour Research and Therapy, 23,* 325-335.

Tennant, C., Hurray, J., & Bebbington, P. (1982). The relation of childhood separation experiences to adult depressive and anxiety states. *British Journal of Psychiatry, 141,* 475-482.

Terhune, W. (1949). The phobic syndrome: A study of 86 patients with phobic reactions. *Archives of Neurology and Psychiatry, 62,* 162-172.

Thoren, P., Asberg, M., Cronholm, B., Jornestedt, L., & Traskman, L. (1980). Clomipramine treatment of obsessive-compulsive disorder: I. A controlled clinical trial. *Archives of General Psychiatry, 37,* 1281-1285.

Thyer, B. A. (1981). Prolonged *in vivo* exposure therapy with a 70-year-old woman. *Journal of Behavior Therapy and Experimental Psychiatry, 12,* 69-71.

Thyer, B. A. (1983). Treating anxiety disorders with exposure therapy. *Social Casework, 64,* 77-82.

Thyer, B. A. (1985a). Audiotaped exposure therapy in a case of obsessional neurosis. *Journal of Behavior Therapy and Experimental Psychiatry, 16,* 271-273.

Thyer, B. A. (1985b). The treatment of phobias in their natural contexts. *Journal of Applied Social Science, 9*(1), 73-83.

Thyer, B. A. (1985c). *Community-based self-help groups in the treatment of agoraphobia.* Manuscript submitted for publication.

Thyer, B. A. (1986). Agoraphobia: A superstitious conditioning perspective. *Psychological Reports, 58,* 95-100.

Thyer, B. A., & Curtis, G. C. (1983). The repeated pretest-posttest single-subject experiment: A new design for empirical clinical practice. *Journal of Behavior Therapy and Experimental Psychiatry, 14,* 311-315.

Thyer, B. A., & Curtis, G. C. (1984). The effects of ethanol intoxication on phobic anxiety. *Behaviour Research and Therapy, 22,* 599-610.

Thyer, B. A., Curtis, G. C., & Fechner, S. (1984). Fear of criticism is not specific to obsessive-compulsive disorder. *Behaviour Research and Therapy, 22,* 77-80.

Thyer, B. A., & Himle, J. (1985). Temporal relationship between panic attack onset and avoidance behavior in agoraphobia with panic attacks. *Behaviour Research and Therapy, 23,* 607-608.

Thyer, B. A., Himle, J., & Curtis, G. C. (1985). Blood-injury-illness phobia: A review. *Journal of Clinical Psychology, 41,* 451-459.

Thyer, B. A., Himle, J., Curtis, G. C., Cameron, O. G., & Nesse, R. M. (1985). A comparison of panic disorder and agoraphobia with panic attacks. *Comprehensive Psychiatry, 26,* 208-214.

Thyer, B. A., Nesse, R. M., Curtis, G. C., & Cameron, O. G. (1985). Agoraphobia: A test of the separation anxiety hypothesis. *Behaviour Research and Therapy, 23,* 75-78.

Thyer, B. A., Nesse, R. M., Cameron, O. G., & Curtis, G. C. (1986). Panic disorder: A test of the separation anxiety hypothesis. *Behaviour Research and Therapy, 24,* 209-211.

Thyer, B. A., & Papsdorf, J. D. (1981). Concurrent validity of the Rational Behavior Inventory. *Psychological Reports, 48,* 255-258.

Thyer, B. A., & Papsdorf, J. D. (1982). Discriminant and concurrent validity of two commonly used measures of test anxiety. *Educational and Psychological Measurement, 42,* 1197-1204.

Thyer, B. A., Papsdorf, J. D., Davis, R., & Vallecorsa, S. (1984). Autonomic correlates of the Subjective Anxiety Scale. *Journal of Behavior Therapy and Experimental Psychiatry, 15*, 3-7.

Thyer, B. A., Papsdorf, J. D., Himle, D. P., McCann, B. S., Caldwell, S., & Wickert, M. (1981). *In-vivo* distraction-coping training in the treatment of test anxiety. *Journal of Clinical Psychology, 37*, 754-764.

Thyer, B. A., Papsdorf, J. D., & Kilgore, S. A. (1983). Relationships between irrational thinking and psychiatric symptomatology. *Journal of Psychology, 113*, 31-34.

Thyer, B. A., Papsdorf, J. D., & Kramer, M. K. (1983). Phobic anxiety and irrational belief systems. *Journal of Psychology, 114*, 145-149.

Thyer, B. A., Papsdorf, J. D., & Wright, P. (1984). Physiological and psychological effects of acute intentional hyperventilation. *Behaviour Research and Therapy, 22*, 587-590.

Thyer, B. A., Parrish, R. T., Curtis, G. C., Cameron, O. G., & Nesse, R. M. (1985). Ages of onset of DSM-III anxiety disorders. *Comprehensive Psychiatry, 26*, 113-122.

Thyer, B. A., Tomlin, P., Curtis, G. C., Cameron, O. G., & Nesse, R. M. (1985). Diagnostic and gender differences in the expressed fears of anxious patients. *Journal of Behavior Therapy and Experimental Psychiatry, 16*, 111-115.

Tinbergen, N. (1951). *The study of instinct.* Oxford: Oxford University Press.

Tippin, J., & Henn, F. A. (1982). Modified leukotomy in the treatment of intractable obsessional neurosis. *American Journal of Psychiatry, 139*, 1601-1603.

Tomlin, P., Thyer, B. A., Curtis, G. C., Nesse, R. M., Cameron, O. G., & Wright, P. (1984). Standardization data of the Fear Survey Schedule based upon patients with a DSM-III anxiety disorder. *Journal of Behavior Therapy and Experimental Psychiatry, 15*, 123-126.

Torgersen, S. (1979). The nature and origin of common phobic fears. *British Journal of Psychiatry, 134*, 343-351.

Torgersen, S. (1983). Genetic factors in anxiety disorders. *Archives of General Psychiatry, 40*, 1085-1089.

Turner, R., Steketee, G. S., & Foa, E. B. (1979). Fear of criticism in washers, checkers and phobics. *Behaviour Research and Therapy, 17*, 79-81.

Turner, S. M., Williams, S. L., Mezzich, J. E., & Beidel, D. C. (1985). *Panic disorder and agoraphobia with panic attacks: Are they distinct diagnostic categories?* Manuscript submitted for publication.

Tyrer, P. (1984). Classification of anxiety. *British Journal of Psychiatry, 144*, 78-83.

Ultee, C. A., Griffioen, D., & Schellekens, J. (1982). The reduction of anxiety in children: A comparison of the effects of "systematic desensitization in *vitro*" and "systematic desensitization *in vivo*." *Behaviour Research and Therapy,20*, 61-67.

Vandereycken, W. (1983). Agoraphobia and marital relationship: Theory, treatment, and research. *Clinical Psychology Review, 3*, 317-338.

Waddell, M. T., Barlow, D. H., & O'Brien, G. T. (1984). A preliminary investigation of cognitive and relaxation treatment of panic disorder: Effects on intense anxiety versus background anxiety. *Behaviour Research and Therapy, 22*, 393-402.

Walters, E. T., & Byrne, J. H. (1983). Associative conditioning of single sensory neurons suggests a cellular mechanism for learning. *Science, 219*, 405-408.

Watson, J. B., & Rayner, R. (1920). Conditioned emotional reactions. *Journal of Experimental Psychology, 3*, 1-14.

Watson, J. P., Mullett, G. E., & Pillay, H. (1973). The effects of prolonged exposure to phobic situations upon agoraphobic patients treated in groups. *Behaviour Research and Therapy, 11*, 531-545.

Weekes, C. (1979). *Simple, effective treatment of agoraphobia.* New York: Bantam.

Wein, K. S., Nelson, R. O., & Odom, J. V. (1975). The relative contributions of reattribution and verbal extinction to the effectiveness of cognitive restructuring. *Behavior Therapy, 6*, 459-474.

Weissman, M. M., Leckman, J. F., Merikangas, K. R., Gammon, G. O., & Prusoff, B. A. (1984). Depression and anxiety disorders in parents and children. *Archives of General Psychiatry, 41*, 845-852.

Westhius, D., Thyer, B. A., & Hudson, W. R. (1986). *Assessing pathological anxiety in clinical practice: The Clinical Anxiety Scale.* Manuscript submitted for publication.

Westphal, C. (1871-72). Die agoraphobie: Eine neuropathische ersheinung. *Arch. fur Psychiatrie und Nervenkrankheiten, 3*, 138-171, 219-221.

Williams, S. L. (1983). Cognitive treatment in the natural environment. *Behavior Therapy, 14*, 299-313.

Wilson, G. D. (1967). Social desirability and sex differences in expressed fear. *Behaviour Research and Therapy, 5*, 136-137.

Wolpe, J. (1952). Experimental neuroses as learned behavior. *British Journal of Psychology, 43*, 243-268.

Wolpe, J. (1958). *Psychotherapy by reciprocal inhibition.* Palo Alto, CA: Stanford University Press.

Wolpe, J. (1964). Behavior therapy in complex neurotic states. *British Journal of Psychiatry, 110*, 28-34.

Wolpe, J. (1969). *The practice of behavior therapy* (2nd ed.). New York: Pergamon.

Wolpe, J. (1982). The dichotomy between classical conditioning and cognitively learned anxiety. *Journal of Behavior Therapy and Experimental Psychiatry, 12*, 35-42.

Wolpe, J., Brady, J. P., Serber, M., Agras, W. S., & Liberman, R. P. (1973). The current status of systematic desensitization. *American Journal of Psychiatry, 130*, 961-965.

Wolpe, J., & Lang, P. (1977). *Manual for the Fear Survey Schedule.* San Francisco: EDITS.

Woodward, R., & Jones, R. (1980). Cognitive restructuring treatment: A controlled trial with anxious patients. *Behaviour Research and Therapy, 18*, 401-407.

Yerkes, R. M., & Yerkes, A. W. (1936). Nature and conditions of avoidance (fear) response in chimpanzees. *Journal of Comparative Psychology, 21*, 53-66.

Zane, M. D., & Milt, H. (1984). *Your phobia.* Washington, DC: American Psychiatric Press.

Zimbardo, P. G. (1977). *Shyness.* New York: Jove Press.

Zitrin, C. M., Klein, D. F., Woerner, M. G., & Ross, D. C. (1983). Treatment of phobias I. Comparison of imipramine hydrochloride and placebo. *Archives of General Psychiatry, 40*, 125-138.

Zitrin, C. M., Woerner, M. G., & Klein, D. F. (1981). Differentiation of panic anxiety from anticipatory anxiety and avoidance behavior. In D. F. Klein & J. Rabkin (Eds.), *Anxiety: New research and changing concepts.* New York: Raven Press.

Zung, W. W. (1971). A rating instrument for anxiety disorders. *Psychosomatics, 12*, 371-379.

ABOUT THE AUTHOR

Bruce A. Thyer is currently Associate Professor of Social Work at Florida State University in Tallahassee. Previously he was a clinical social worker with the Anxiety Disorders Program of the Department of Psychiatry at the University of Michigan Hospitals, where he was extensively involved in the treatment of patients suffering from anxiety disorders; research into the etiology, psychobiology, and management of pathological anxiety; and served as a faculty member with the University of Michigan Medical School. He is the author of numerous publications in the field of anxiety disorders and has been a guest editor (with associates) of special issues of *The Psychiatric Clinics of North America* and the *Journal of Social Service Research*.